Taylor Wessing
PHOTO PORTRAIT PRIZE
23

AF394758

NATIONAL PORTRAIT GALLERY

Contents

Director's Foreword

This is an exciting time for the *Taylor Wessing Photo Portrait Prize*, following the reopening of the National Portrait Gallery in June, earlier this year, after the largest transformation since our building opening in 1896. We are thrilled to welcome the competition's exhibition back into the Gallery itself. Highlighting leading approaches to contemporary photography, the Prize showcases an array of artists – from emerging photographers, to established professionals.

This year, 5,020 submissions were received, by 1,785 photographers. Attracting entries from around the world, photographers from 59 different countries submitted works. This year we have also introduced the Taylor Wessing Photographic Commission, which will result in a new portrait for the Gallery's photographs collection. Alongside my fellow judges, we made a final selection of 58 works including 5 prizewinners. We have awarded a joint third place prize, testament to this year's high quality of submissions. I'd like to congratulate all the prizewinners: Alexandre Silberman, Gilleam Trapenberg, Jake Green, Carl Francois van der Linde and Serena Brown.

This year's submissions were remarkable. My thanks go out to my fellow judges Campbell Addy, Caleb Azumah Nelson, Sabina Jaskot-Gill and Karen McQuaid, for their invaluable insight and collaboration within this process.

Our In Focus Photographer this year is Hassan Hajjaj, a Moroccan-British artist who lives and works between London and Marrakech. His vibrant portraits incorporate references to African studio portraiture and Western pop art, mixing traditional Moroccan fabrics and motifs with contemporary streetwear and maximalist styling, to explore his experience of living between British and North African cultures.

I would like to thank the staff of the National Portrait Gallery, Grade Design for their work on the exhibition catalogue, and White Wall Company for brilliantly managing the judging process. I would also like to recognise Professor Anna Fox and the Fast Forward research project, as well as artist and curator Bindi Vora, for their advice on increasing access to the competition's call for entries.

We are thankful to Taylor Wessing's contribution to the success of this competition and exhibition.

Nicholas Cullinan
Director, National Portrait Gallery, London

Sponsor's Foreword

In its sixteenth year, the *Taylor Wessing Photo Portrait Prize* has once again exceeded expectations, continuing to showcase talent from across the world. This year, a number of important updates have been introduced to the competition with the aim of removing barriers to participation and encouraging entries from under-represented countries. These changes are aligned with the Gallery's ambition to increase the accessibility of the competition, and have been made with our support. We are delighted to see their impact.

We are also excited to support the new Taylor Wessing Photographic Commission, which will result in a new work being created for the Gallery's permanent collection.

The wide-ranging participation of artists from across the globe, both amateur and professional, shows the growing popularity and prestige of the Prize – of which we are so proud to be the sponsor.

I hope that you enjoy the images selected for the 2023 exhibition and will join me in congratulating all of the photographers whose portraits are featured.

Shane Gleghorn
Managing Partner, Taylor Wessing

The Prizes

The *Taylor Wessing Photo Portrait Prize* is open to photographers from around the world, aged 18 or over. Exhibited annually at the National Portrait Gallery, London, the Prize showcases talented photographers, both professional and amateur. The winner of the competition receives £15,000, with second prize receiving £3,000 and third prize £2,000. In addition, this year the National Portrait Gallery has launched a new £8,000 Taylor Wessing Photographic Commission, which will see a photographer selected to create a work for the Gallery's collection.

First Prize

Alexandre Silberman

Silberman's photograph, *Diena*, captures a face-to-face encounter in the light and shade of Georges-Valbon park, near Paris (p.8).

Second Prize

Gilleam Trapenberg

Exploring the idea of home, Trapenberg intimately photographs a mother and son in *Kisha and LaDarayon* (p.10).

Third Prize

Jake Green

In his portrait of Shaun Ryder, Green creates humour and intrigue through a striking composition (p.12).

Carl Francois van der Linde

Van der Linde's *Chotu Lal Upside-down* looks at wrestling culture at Great Khali's CWE Academy in Jalandhar, rural India (p.14).

**Taylor Wessing
Photographic Commission**

Serena Brown

In *me nana fie*, Brown warmly photographs her sister as they travel to visit family in Accra, Ghana (p.16).

The Judges

Campbell Addy
Photographer and Filmmaker
To see an array of photographers creating art and telling stories is what I love about the medium of photography – I am moved and most definitely inspired!

Caleb Azumah Nelson
Novelist and Photographer
It was beautiful to see such a presence of storytelling and dedication to composition through the photographers' work.

Nicholas Cullinan
Director, National Portrait Gallery and
Chair of Panel
I am proud to see the Prize return to the Gallery, after our three-year redevelopment project, with such an accomplished range of portraits.

Sabina Jaskot-Gill
Senior Curator, Photographs,
National Portrait Gallery
I enjoyed looking closely at the physical prints, and appreciating all the carefully considered nuances of colour, tone and scale.

Karen McQuaid
Senior Curator, Photographer's Gallery
The outstanding finalists attest to the myriad of fascinating ways photographers navigate social, personal and psychological space with their subjects.

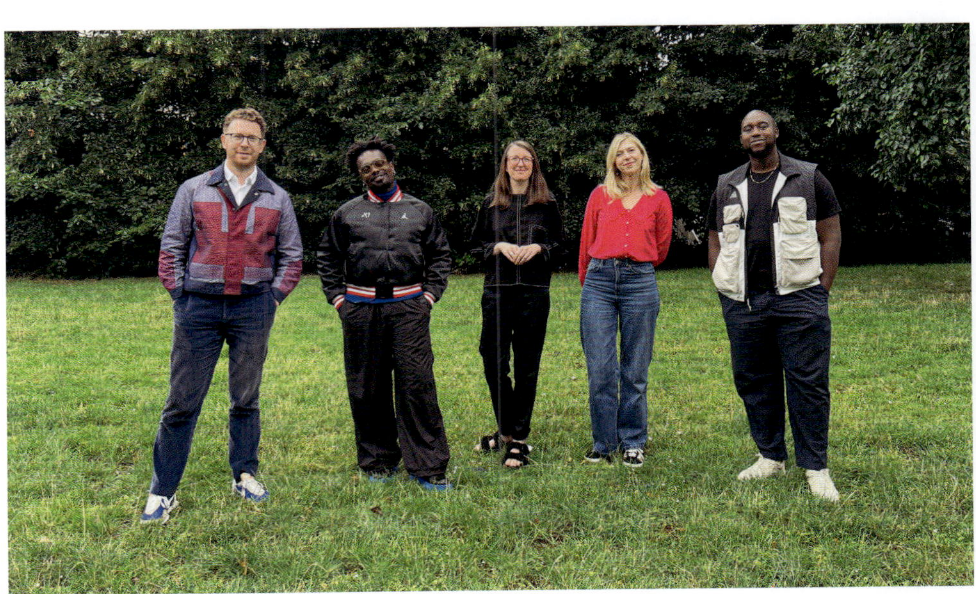

The judges, July 2023. Left to right: Nicholas Cullinan, Campbell Addy, Karen McQuaid, Sabina Jaskot-Gill, Caleb Azumah Nelson

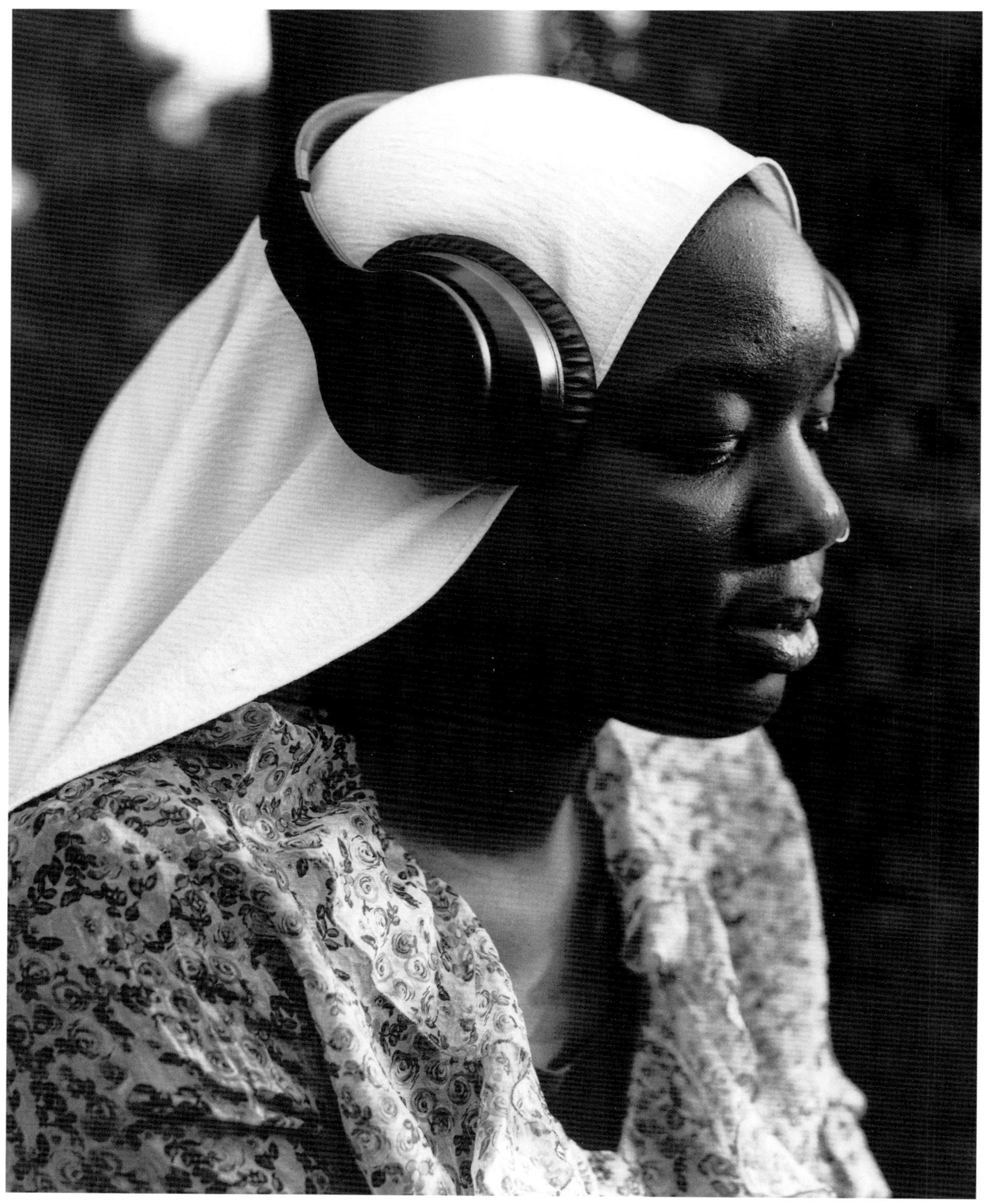

Alexandre Silberman
Diena, July 2022
From the series *NATURE*
Gelatin silver print

First Prize
Alexandre Silberman

Alexandre Silberman arrived at photography 'relatively late', having first established a career as a television and film director. Born in 1983 in Dortmund, Germany, his family moved to Lyon, France, when he was 3 years old, where he later studied philosophy at the city's university. 'Photography is a passion' for Silberman, who first started exhibiting his work in 2016, noting that 'it offered more freedom, allowing opportunities to shoot spontaneously and work alone after years of directing large crews and productions.'

For a number of years Silberman has been photographing the suburb of Seine-Saint-Denis, to the north east of Paris, one of the youngest and most culturally diverse areas of France, but also one of the poorest. His series *Differences & Repetitions* (2019–21) documents Seine-Saint-Denis' urban landscapes alongside portraits of its inhabitants.

Although now based in Paris, Silberman grew up in the suburbs of Lyon, and acknowledges how this generates a sense of *ennui* that can be felt in his images: 'What I experienced in the suburbs in my youth was boredom, there was nothing to do, and maybe in my work, I am aware of this feeling.' He cites the American photographer Gregory Halpern as a source of inspiration, in particular Halpern's ability to 'create compositions that narrate a silent story.'

Silberman returned to Seine-Saint-Denis in 2022 for an ongoing series, *NATURE*, which includes portraits taken in Georges-Valbon park, or La Courneuve park as it is also known, one of the largest green spaces around Paris. For Silberman, the park is 'rooted in the utopian aesthetics of the 1970s, but at the same time it is very authentic in its approach, communicating a true spirit of nature to its visitors,' which are mostly comprised of the local community.

Diena was 'an apparition,' Silberman remembers; 'light shining on her figure.' It was the first time the 23-year-old had been formally photographed, but she readily agreed. 'I saw her from very far away, sitting alone in the park, carrying a suitcase and a bouquet of dried flowers, wearing a long white veil, illuminated by sunlight.'

He shot twenty photographs with two rolls of film, but, while preparing to leave, Silberman looked back at his subject and realised he 'had made a mistake with his composition.' With only two frames left, he knew he had to take a close-up shot.

Having already photographed Georges-Valbon park in colour, this time he shot in black and white, being 'more interested in capturing light and shade than the green of the park.' His prize-winning portrait of Diena was shot in strong, direct sunlight, allowing Silberman to 'sculpt with light.' The monochrome palette lends a dreamlike quality to the work, but details within the portrait, such as Diena's nose ring, floral blouse and headphones, bring it into the present.

Silberman works exclusively with analogue photography, using a medium format Pentax 6×7 camera for this series. He recognises that with smaller cameras you can be 'very spontaneous, and capture a moment on the street,' but 'medium format forces me to stop and think and compose an image.' He also notes that larger cameras are more 'visible,' which 'sparks more conversations with people, and leads to more portraits.'

Describing the appeal of portraiture, Silberman explains, 'I love the face-to-face relationship with a person. It only lasts a few moments, but creates a strong connection with the model, an intense relationship. They are giving you a part of themselves,' he concludes, 'it's a mark of trust.'

Interview by Sabina Jaskot-Gill

Second Prize
Gilleam Trapenberg

Gilleam Trapenberg's work reflects on 'the imaging and imagining of the Caribbean.' Born in 1991 in Curaçao, a Dutch Caribbean island about 40 miles north of Venezuela, Trapenberg now uses photography to explore a more nuanced understanding of daily life in the country he grew up in. He is particularly interested in exploring the disconnect between representations of Caribbean islands in contemporary visual culture and the lived reality of everyday life for the islands' inhabitants.

Trapenberg's interest in photography began as a teenager, when he borrowed his mother's camera on vacations, and became interested in the technical aspects of the medium. At the age of 19, he moved to the Netherlands to study photography at the Royal Academy of Art in The Hague, where, he explains, 'a new world opened up to me.'

This prize-winning portrait was made on the island of Saint Martin, part of the Leeward Islands of the Lesser Antilles, which he frequently visited with his father as a child. Trapenberg drives a car around an island until he spots something to photograph – people, landscapes, details of objects that catch his eye: 'I see my images as pieces of a puzzle, fragmented parts with which I try to tell a coherent story.'

'I met Kisha one day while driving past her house. She was standing on the side of the road, and I wanted to know her story,' he recalls. Trapenberg first photographed Kisha in 2018 and returned frequently to photograph her family; he admits that forming such a bond with an individual is unusual in his practice. This portrait was taken in early 2023, in front of Kisha's grandmother's house, and Trapenberg 'liked the ordinariness, the banality of the image.'

Trapenberg used a Mamiya RZ67, a heavy medium format camera, with a tripod and waist-level viewfinder, which changes the dynamic of a portrait sitting: 'When I'm focusing the lens, I'm looking down into my camera, so suddenly there is a moment of reflection for the sitter. There is a slight moment where they drop their guard, and that's when I take the picture.'

Kisha is pictured with her youngest son, LaDarayon, who was 10 years old at the time. 'He just stood in front of his mother, and she hugged him, and I knew right away, this is a beautiful portrait,' Trapenberg remembers. 'It felt like a mother holding onto her son before he enters adolescence,' but also, he suggests, a son beginning to outgrow his mother's embrace.

For Trapenberg, the portrait also invokes a dilemma faced by some young people across the Caribbean islands, who have to decide whether to move away from their families to pursue studies abroad. Having lived now in the Netherlands for 12 years, Trapenberg experienced this predicament first-hand. He finds himself occupying 'a liminal space' between the two countries, with 'a longing for the island that I left behind.' His photography up to this point, he acknowledges, has been 'a way for me to try and understand that. I realised that the work is as much about me as it is about the people I'm photographing.'

Portraits of Kisha were included in the series *This Surely Must Be Paradise*, exhibited at the Stedelijk Museum, Amsterdam, in 2020. Trapenberg is now incorporating his work on Saint Martin and Curaçao into a larger series, *Currents*, which he hopes will evolve into a book, focused more broadly on 'the constant flow of people to and from the Caribbean islands.'

Interview by Sabina Jaskot-Gill

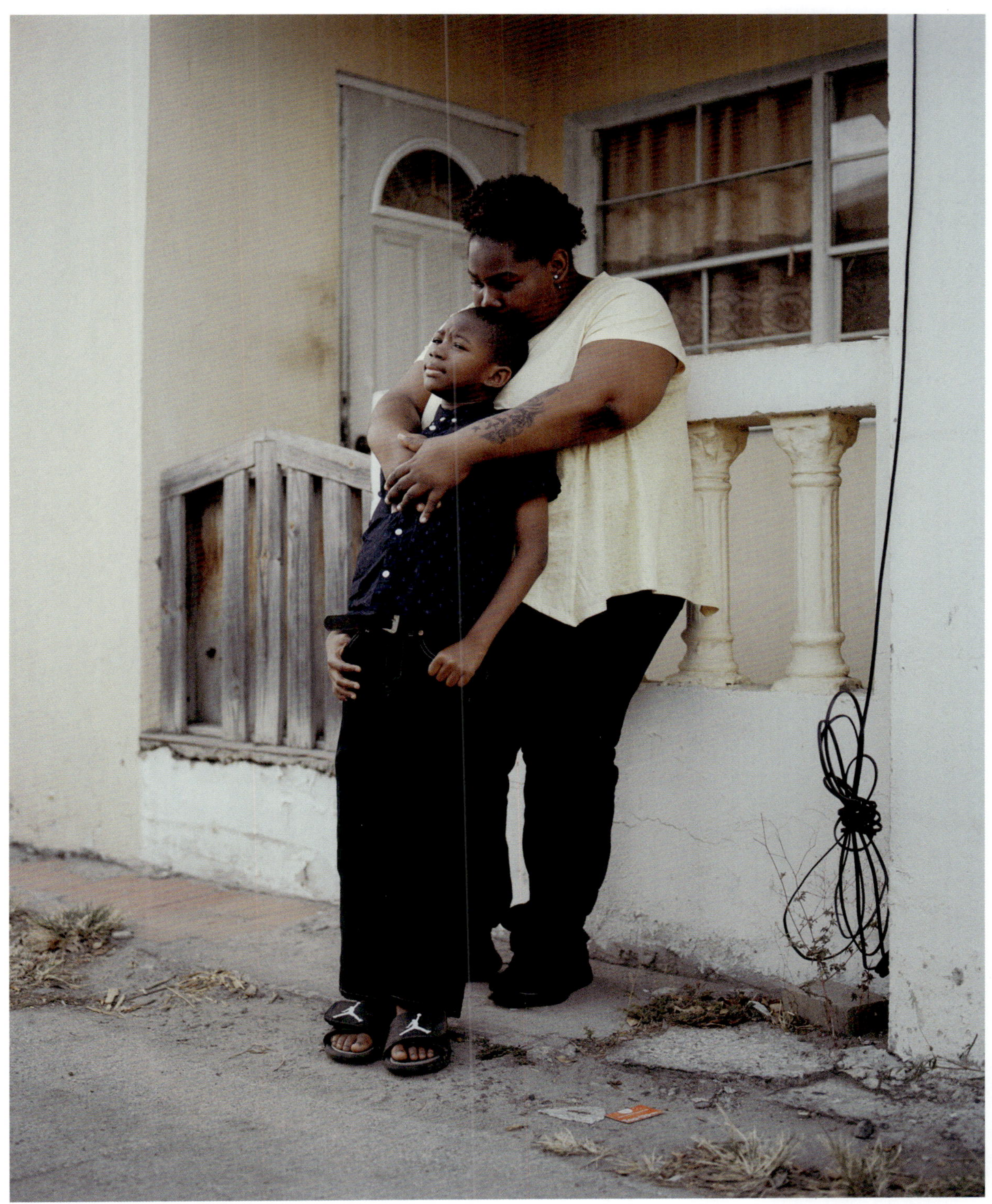

Gilleam Trapenberg
Kisha and LaDarayon, March 2023
From the series *Currents*
Inkjet print

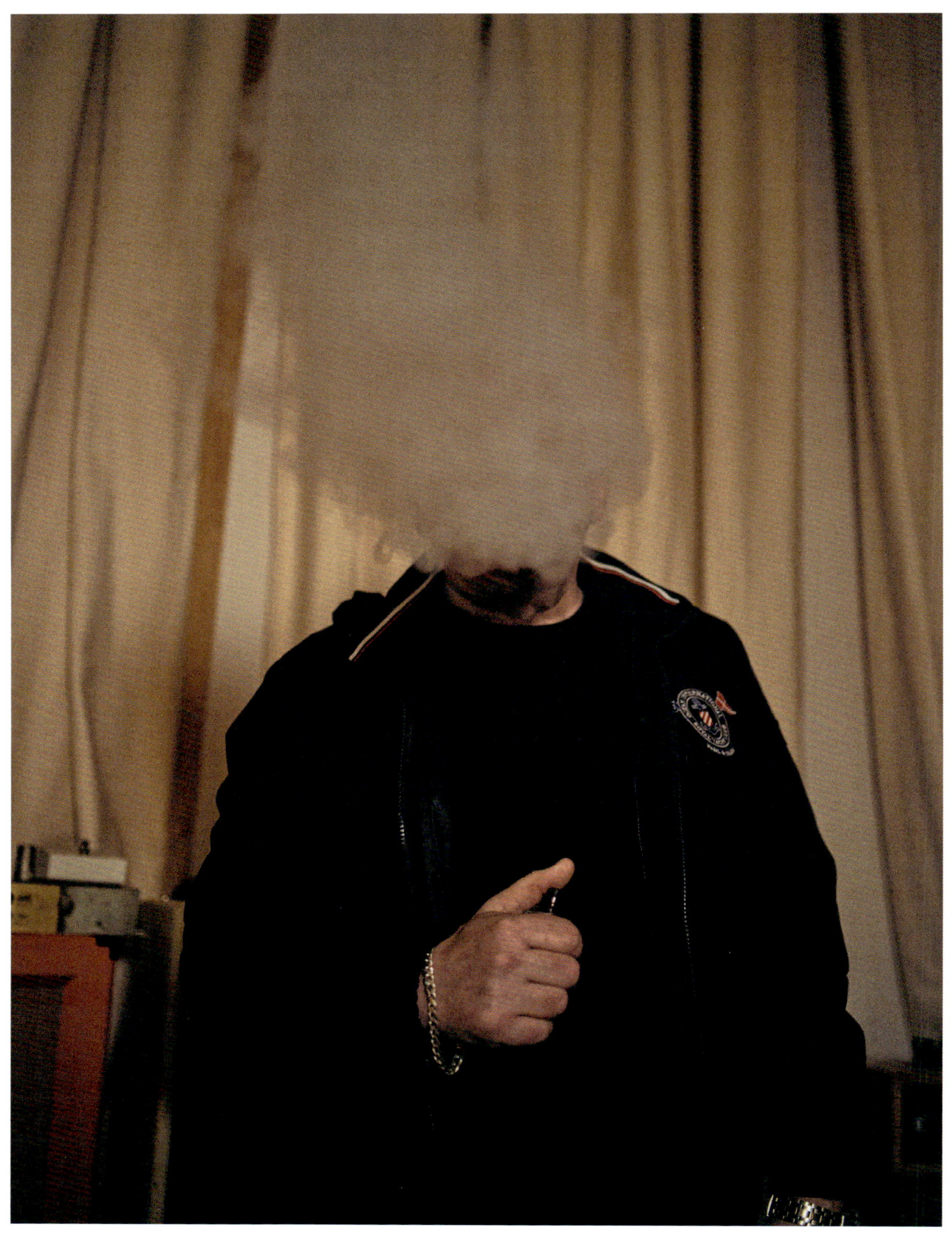

Jake Green
Shaun Ryder, May 2023
Inkjet print

Third Prize
Jake Green

Jake Green, a born-and-bred East Ender, is passionate about his community. In Leytonstone where he lives, he has helped to establish an arts community centre. It is this altruistic connection with people and a love of home that influences his photography. 'I've grown up in East London. I've got this strong, deep-rooted love of it. I express myself through my community – it's something I have that differentiates me from any other artists.'

Collaboration and the sharing of ideas has always been key to developing his lens-based interactions. Articulating this passion has been aided by ongoing conversations with creative director and writer Gem Fletcher, which have helped Green to 'relate and focus.' He also cites his good friend, fellow photographer Rinchen Ato, as a great source of inspiration and encouragement. As a teen, Green experimented with an SLR camera, and on an art foundation course at London Guildhall, he was always drawn to the darkroom. A year working in a processing lab solidified his appreciation of colour and print.

His prize-winning portrait is of Shaun Ryder, former lead singer of 'Madchester's' Happy Mondays. Green explains that an honest and disarming conversation preceded the musician's suggestion that Green capture him vaping – a surreal experience for the photographer. Ryder's head disappeared behind a cloud of smoke in a moment of self-obliteration, allowing for a humorous and intriguing portrait of a once world-famous pop star.

During the sitting, Green found himself to have a rapport with Ryder, which is something, along with an imaginative element, he thinks is key to a successful portrait. He photographed digitally with a Fuji camera but his use of manual lenses, whether working in analogue or digital, offers control and consistency. The editing process, which follows a frenzied working period, is thrilling – 'no matter how tired I am, I'll sit down with my edit and I just go. I just love that process.' The revelation of what has been captured, the feeling of the 'right' image, Green believes, results from a feeling of connection with the moment.

Passions and rituals run throughout Green's work. The living history and daily rituals of East London pie and mash shops resulted in a book and film project, while his global photography series *Drink My Sweat* documents the lives of people working in the international coffee industry, connecting the people that drink it with those who produce it.

Green's most recent, ongoing project is based around his local football ground, Leyton Orient, where he worked as a teen. This familial territory drives his understanding of the players' and supporters' passion and energy. Through his portraits of these figures, Green seeks to demystify representations of masculinity and to challenge 'the stereotypical representation of male football fans and "typical" East Londoners,' a subject that is close to home.

Interview by Clare Freestone

Third Prize
Carl Francois van der Linde

Having submitted all the works in his *Our Leader* series to this year's competition, Carl Francois van der Linde was surprised by the two photographs that the judges selected. He felt that his other portraits of the wrestlers at Great Khali's CWE Academy in Jalandhar in rural India, pictured in character and ready for 'showtime,' may have been more eye-catching. However, it was his behind-the-scenes portraits that were chosen – *Chotu Lal Upside-down* winning third prize, and *Dev Dangi* selected to be exhibited (p.57). He reflects, 'it makes you question where as a photographer your strength lies and what best tells the story?'

Van der Linde was born in 1993 in South Africa, where he later studied economics. However, in 2016, soon after picking up a point-and-shoot camera, he realised that this art form could be the 'vessel' by which to see the world. 'It opened more doors for me in terms of what is possible in exploring an interest. As a kid going through *National Geographic*, I always thought you have to be a scientist to go into the Amazon, but photographers can share the same anthropological philosophy.'

He taught himself analogue photography at a time when there was a global resurrection in the use of film, and was inspired by photographers including Pieter Hugo and Max Pinckers, who made him question, 'how did they gain access to hard-to-reach or fringe subjects? How much red tape did they cut through?' At the same time as this, he studied the 'quality of the image, the depth, the colours, and the contrast,' to aid his 'journey of self-discovery.'

However complex the image, for van der Linde it is the long process preceding the single capture – the pursuit of sitters from places across the world, building the confidence of people from different socio economic situations – that is most challenging. The seed for his series *Our Leader* was an online meme of the Great Khali, the first Indian-born WWE World Heavyweight Champion, who has millions of fans across the globe. A wrestling fan as a child, van der Linde reached out via social media, proposing he profiled 30 wrestlers at Khali's academy. A year of back-and-forth communication resulted in a three-week shoot.

The vast amount of organisation that precedes the sitting drives the intensity and success of the shoot. Van der Linde describes *kayfabe* (the staged performance of wrestling) and bizarre pranks often filmed to increase wrestlers' social media followings, from which he gleaned the image of Chotu Lal, hanging upside down from a tree, flanked by the flesh of his fellow wrestlers. 'I think it's part of the appeal of that photo. You don't know what's going on.'

Van der Linde uses a medium format film camera with natural light and a strobe if required, but always works alone: 'very simple. I travel with one bag. That feels brave, doesn't it, these days? But that's the beauty. That's the thrill of it.' As a storyteller and an avid observer, he also authors the texts to accompany his work when the opportunity allows. Nominated one of *PhotoVogue*'s Next Great Fashion Image Makers in 2022, his drive to evoke emotion and share daily rituals from across the world in photographic form is palpable; 'you have to be conscious your ego doesn't take over, but you have to harness its powers.'

Interview by Clare Freestone

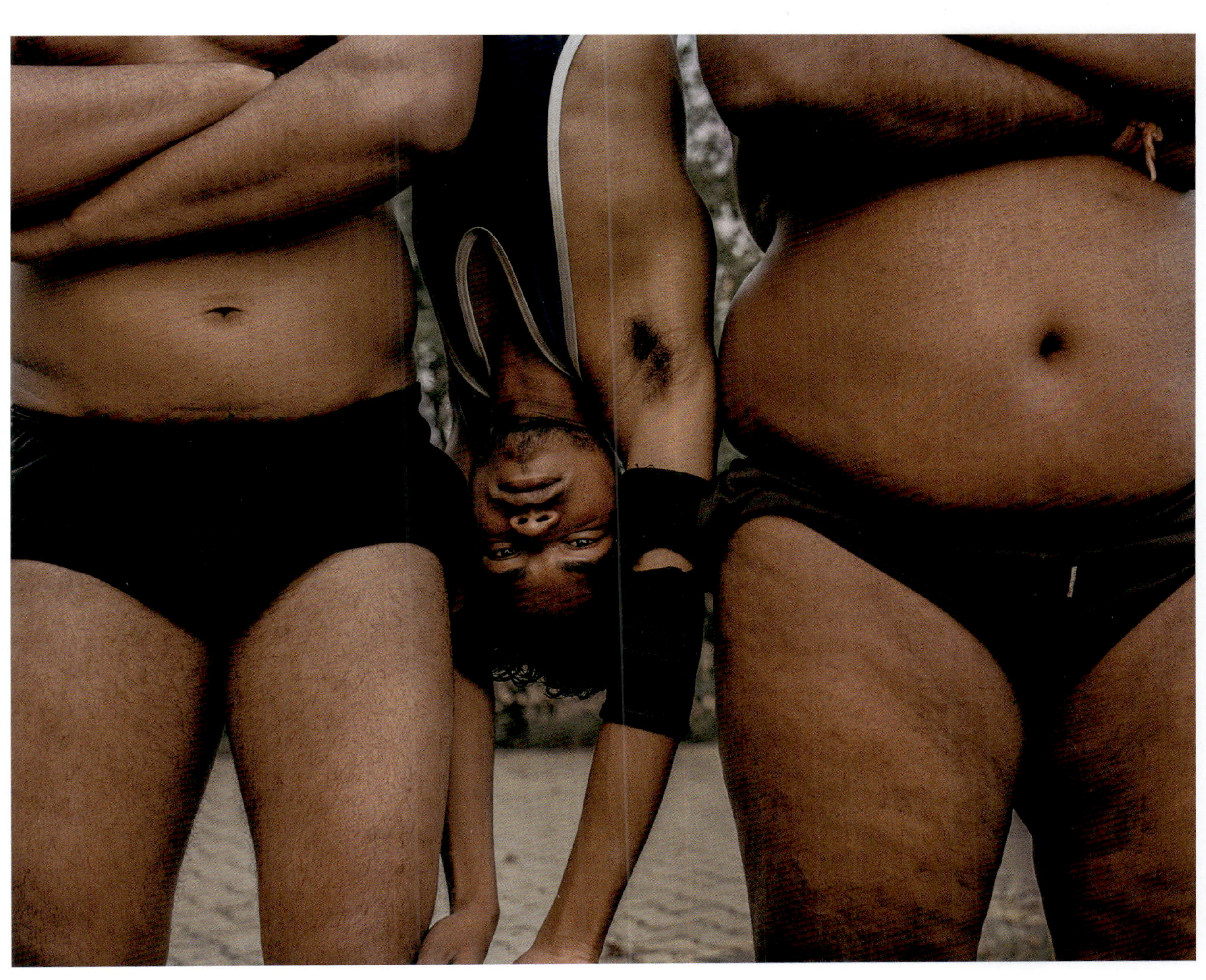

Carl Francois van der Linde
Chotu Lal Upside-down, February 2023
From the series *Our Leader*
Inkjet print

Taylor Wessing Photographic Commission Serena Brown

The recipient of the inaugural Taylor Wessing Photographic Commission is London-based photographer Serena Brown, whose honest, joyful and authentic portraits celebrate and uplift her community.

Born in 1997 to Scottish-Ghanaian parents in west London, she grew up surrounded by a close group of family and friends – 'a lovely little bubble of Ghana' – which 'created a sense of working-class community,' she explains, 'and being proud of where you're from.'

Brown was interested in photography from a young age. 'It's probably a little clichéd,' she acknowledges, 'but I have always been the person with the camera in their hands.' Though, she admits, 'I don't think I realised what a career in photography could be.'

Moving to Cornwall to study photography at Falmouth University was 'a shock.' Brown remembers 'feeling othered' for the first time: 'I stood out a lot more and I was conscious of myself and the things I said. I had to explain myself a little more.' The experience has translated into her practice: 'it steered me on the path of knowing that I really want to make work that is going to be shared and understood by my community.'

One such project was *Back a Yard*, her final year project, which looked at the appropriation of black and Asian working class youth culture within fashion. The 2020 series *Class of Covid-19* 'gave a voice to young people' during the pandemic. She elaborates, 'I'm really passionate about being able to offer a platform to people who aren't usually given opportunities to be photographed.'

Last year, Brown visited her family in Accra, Ghana, returning for the first time since she was 2. She travelled with her younger sister, Chloe, who had never visited the country before. 'It felt like such a beautiful homecoming. We've been raised so closely to our Ghanaian culture, this was the final piece of the puzzle, experiencing the place for ourselves.'

Brown was wary of documenting the country 'through my London lens,' she explains. 'It made sense to begin the work in the confines of my grandma's house, because I spent so much time there,' and she began photographing the people who dropped into *me nana fie* ('my grandma's house' in the Ghanaian dialect, Twi) – friends, family and street sellers all feature. 'It's very much in the culture to always be ready for guests,' she explains, 'the community is always in and out of each other's lives. You're never alone.'

This portrait of the photographer's sister came about 'organically and spontaneously.' It features a young boy they had recently met – Kojo, the son of her grandma's driver – with a cheeky expression, peeking out from behind her sister on the porch. The work is typical of Brown's style. 'I like to photograph people in their authentic surroundings,' she says – 'stripped-back portraits with natural light.' She uses a handheld medium format camera, preferring the slower pace of film photography, which does not allow for instant image review during a shoot.

Brown has been enjoying a 'post-Covid freelance career,' collaborating with brands including Nike, Pepsi and England Football, and producing commissioned portraits for the *New York Times* and *Elle* magazine. Her work also featured in a recent group exhibition, *Women on Women*; for Brown, this was 'a celebration of the community that I've started to build as a photographer, and an opportunity to note how far I've come.' Having graduated from Falmouth in 2018, she will be returning to the university in 2024 as a photography tutor – 'it's a nice full circle moment,' she admits.

Interview by Sabina Jaskot-Gill

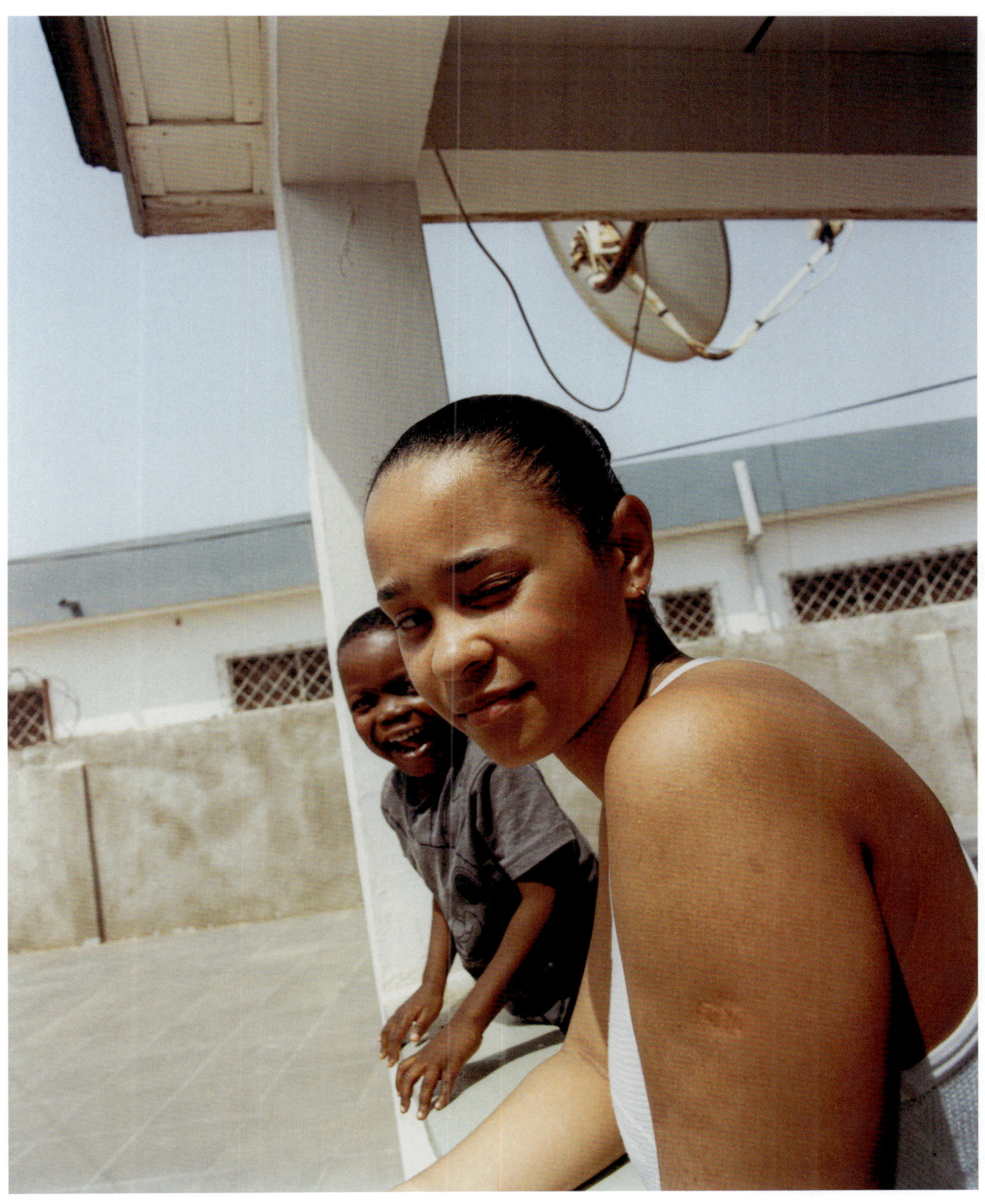

Serena Brown
me nana fie, March 2022
Chromogenic print

Exhibitors

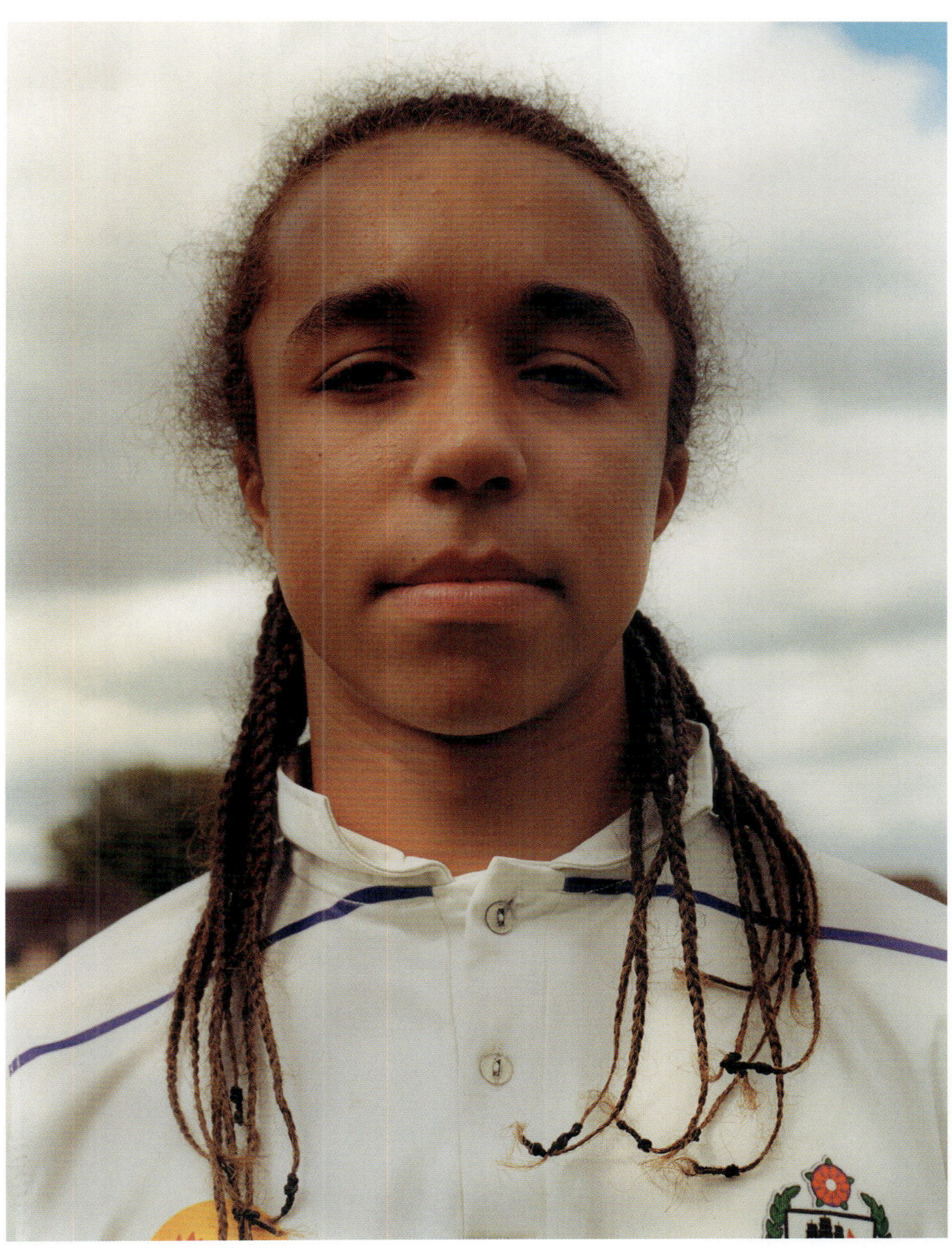

Vivek Vadoliya

Jacob, July 2022
From the series *The Face: Youth Cricket Study*
Chromogenic print

Jacob has been playing for the South West Manchester Cricket Club since he was 5 years old. Now a teenager, he supports the West Indies and Lancaster cricket teams. In the wake of allegations of racism at Yorkshire County Cricket Club, British-Indian photographer and director Vivek Vadoliya was commissioned by *The Face* magazine to explore how a new generation of junior players are bringing a broad, culturally diverse demographic to the sport. As Jacob noted, 'everyone can play, everyone should be welcome to play.'

Rory Payne

Nana Dancing Queen (Tracey Booker), April 2023
Nana Turtle (Marjorie Millar), April 2023
From the series *Nanashire – Nana's Against Fracking*
Chromogenic prints

Nana's Against Fracking are fighting to protect future generations from the effects of fracking and fossil fuels. British photographer Rory Payne was commissioned by the *Conversationalist* to photograph the activist group at a fracking site in Blackpool where they had been protesting for over 1,000 days. Payne met his sitters on the day of the shoot and quickly learnt the stories of their 'nana names.' Tracey had been styled 'Nana Dancing Queen' by Dame Vivienne Westwood after they had danced together to ABBA music at the gates of the Preston New Road fracking site.

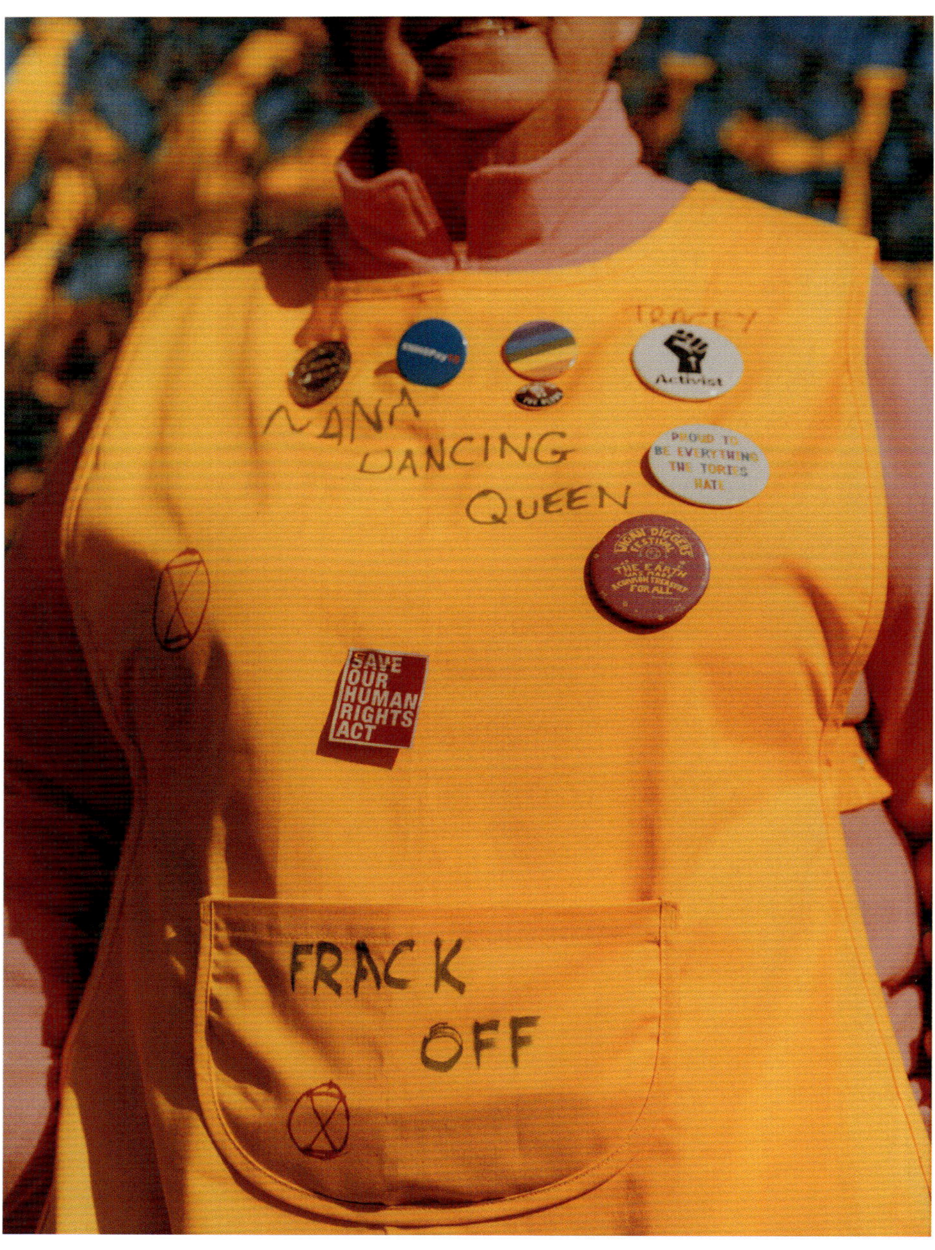

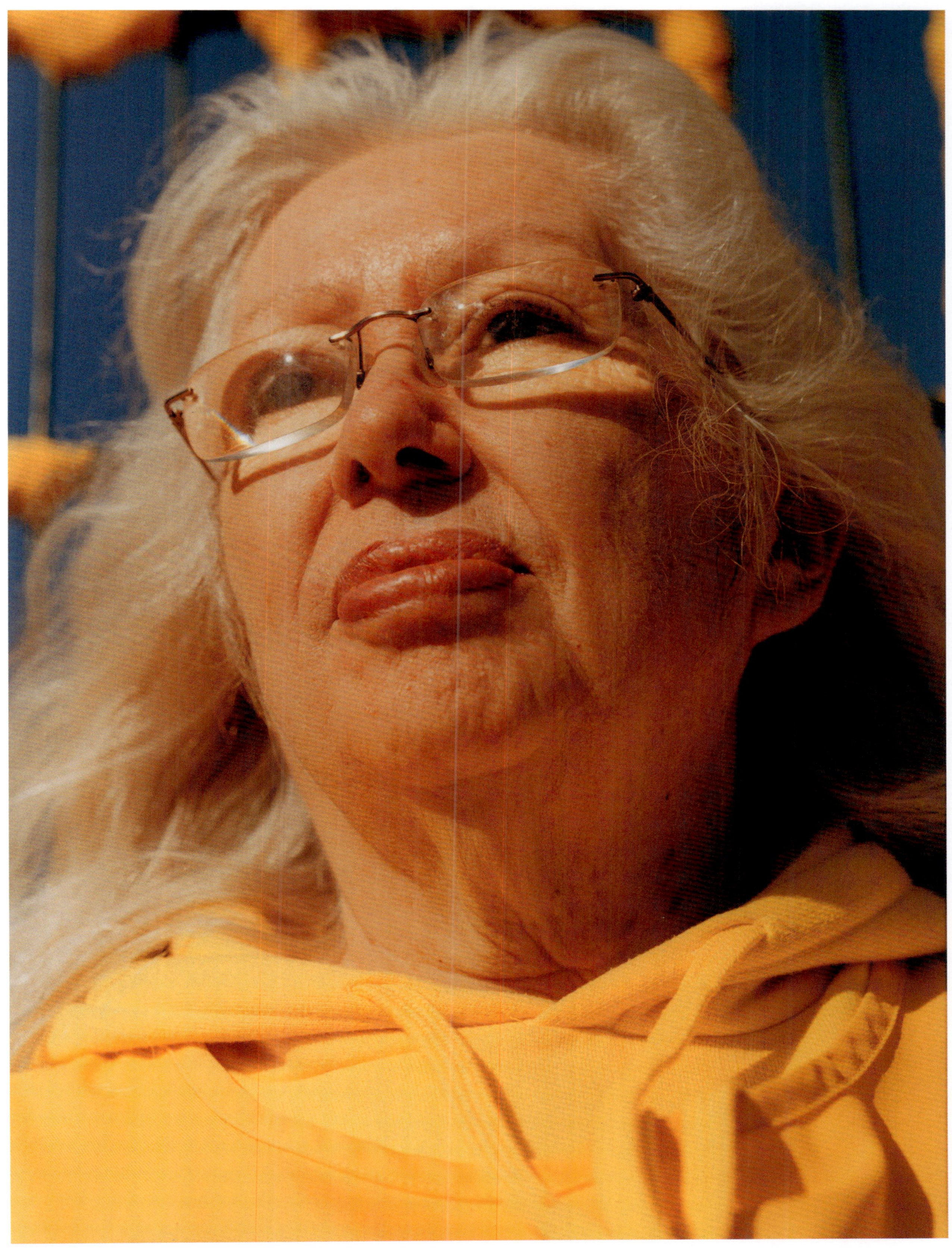

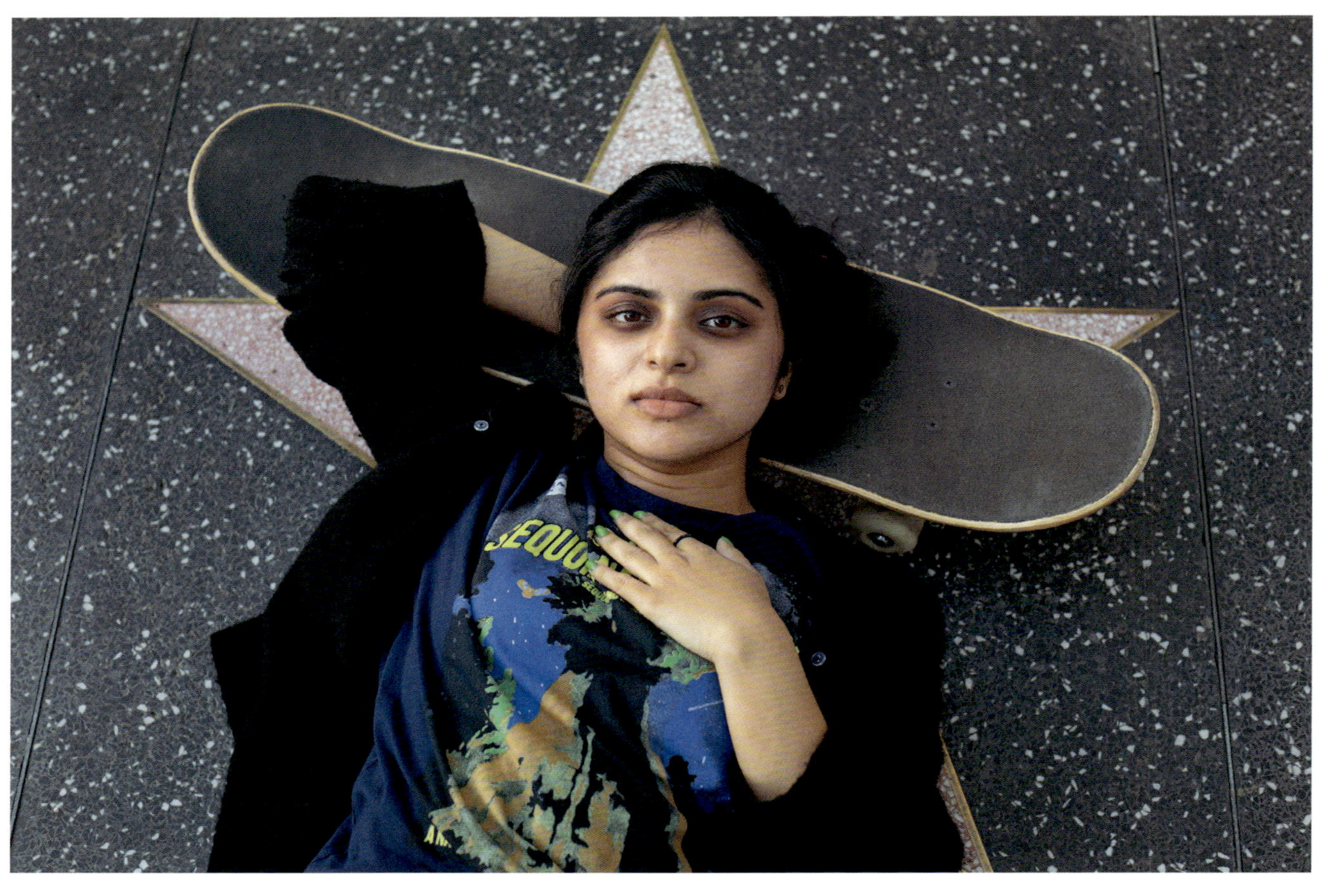

Mahtab Hussain
Rida Qureshi, October 2022
From the series *Muslims in America – LA Chapter*
Inkjet print

Lying on a Hollywood star, her head resting upon her skateboard, Rida's direct gaze presents a strong and assured identity. Her portrait is part of an ongoing series, *Muslims in America*, begun by British portrait photographer Mahtab Hussain to humanise the experience of fellow Western Muslims and challenge stereotypes the community faces. Responding to the poor visibility of Muslims in American art and media, he has so far visited New York, Los Angeles and Baltimore to create street portraits informed by conversations with sitters about their experiences.

Ruth Samuels
Group Portrait, March 2023
From the series *The Beholder*
Inkjet print

British photographer Ruth Samuels seeks to amplify marginalised voices and empower women through her work. Her series challenges societal conventions of perceived beauty, celebrating women who for too long have 'been made to feel inferior.' Samuels explains, 'as a black woman, I've found myself feeling emotionally weighed down by a lot of what I see and hear online: our features are "not delicate enough," we're "too muscular," "too dark," our natural textured hair is "undesirable."' The portrait of models Renita, Chloe and Caitlyn is an invitation by Samuels 'to find beauty in places' that may have been 'previously missed.'

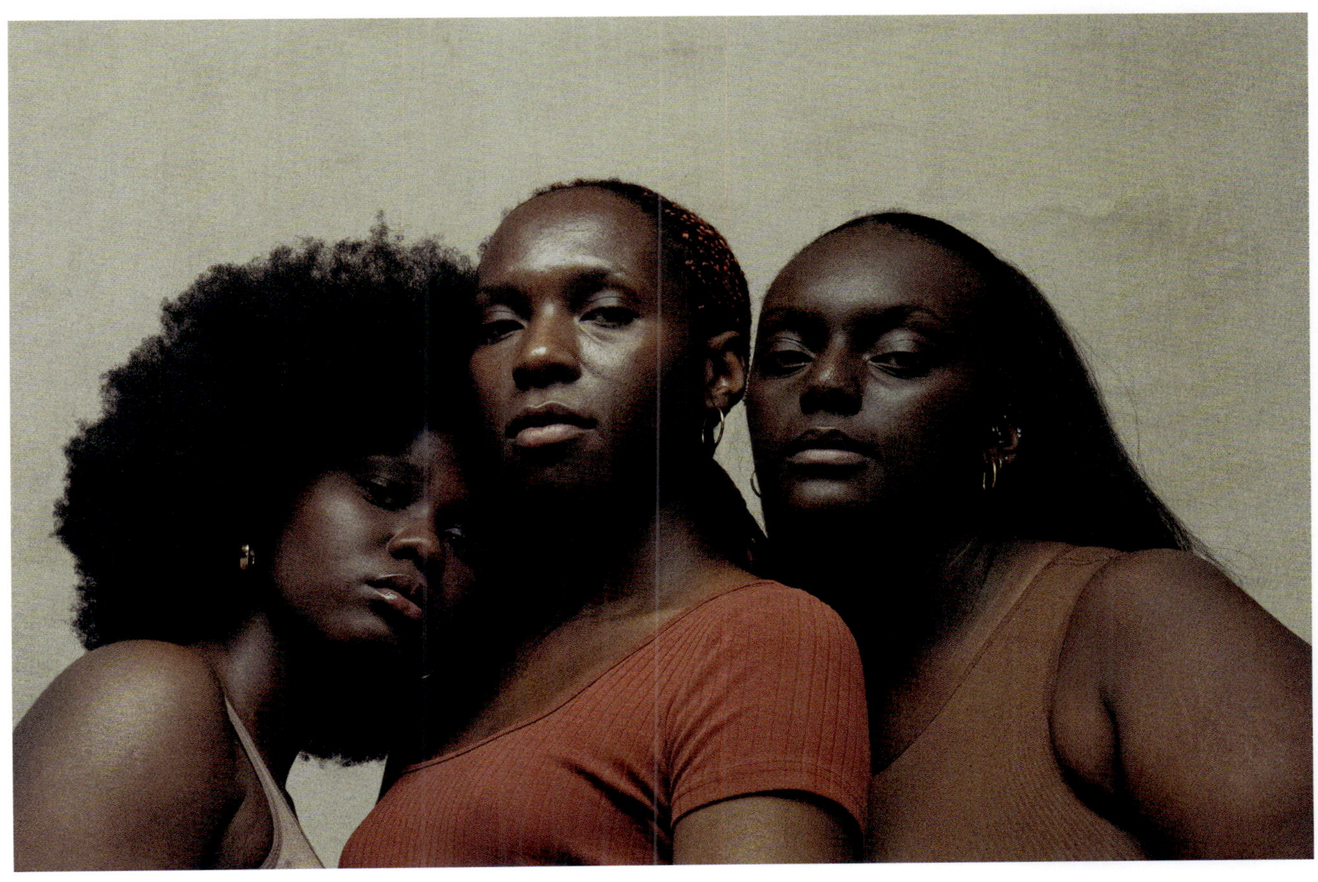

Sukhy Hullait
Gloria, August 2022
From the series *All The Rage*
Inkjet print

British photographer Sukhy Hullait has lived in the neighbouring London areas of Peckham and East Dulwich for most of his adult life. Hullait uses his camera to explore his neighbourhood and capture the unique, vibrant spirits of the people he meets. Gloria has lived in Peckham all her life, and talks proudly about her love of gardening. She grows plants and flowers outside her home, on the doorsteps of neighbours, by lampposts and in any other spaces she can find, driven by her desire to spread a little joy.

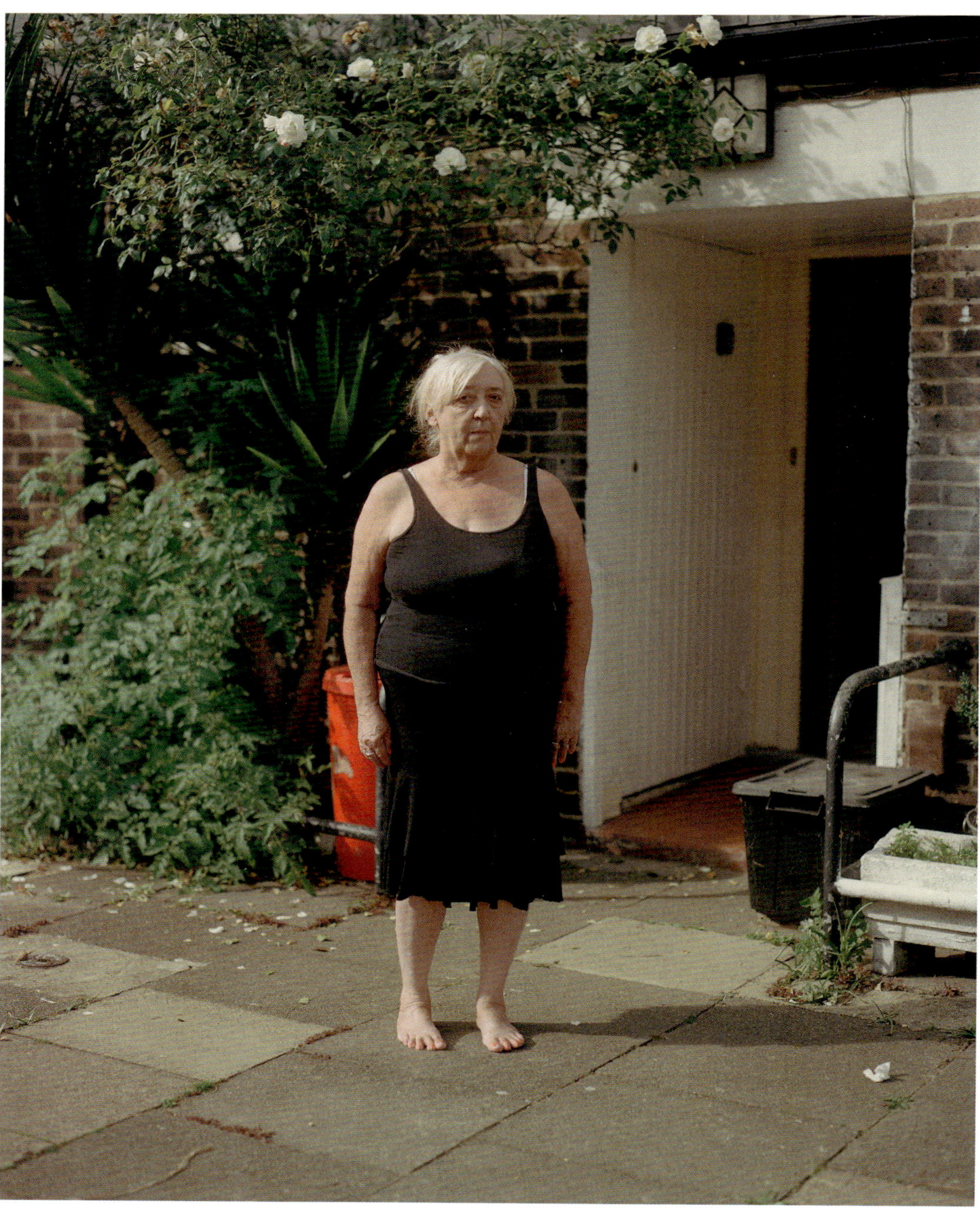

Alexander Parkyn-Smith

Zhoon Kungoi, Kyrgyzstan, June 2022
Inkjet print

While working on a project researching women entrepreneurs in Central Asia, British visual anthropologist Alexander Parkyn-Smith lived with a family in south Kyrgyzstan. The son was showing him around the family's smallholding just as an electric storm rolled in from the mountains. Parkyn-Smith captured the boy's ageless expression as he watched the raindrops fall, the camera's flash illuminating the vibrant roses in the foreground.

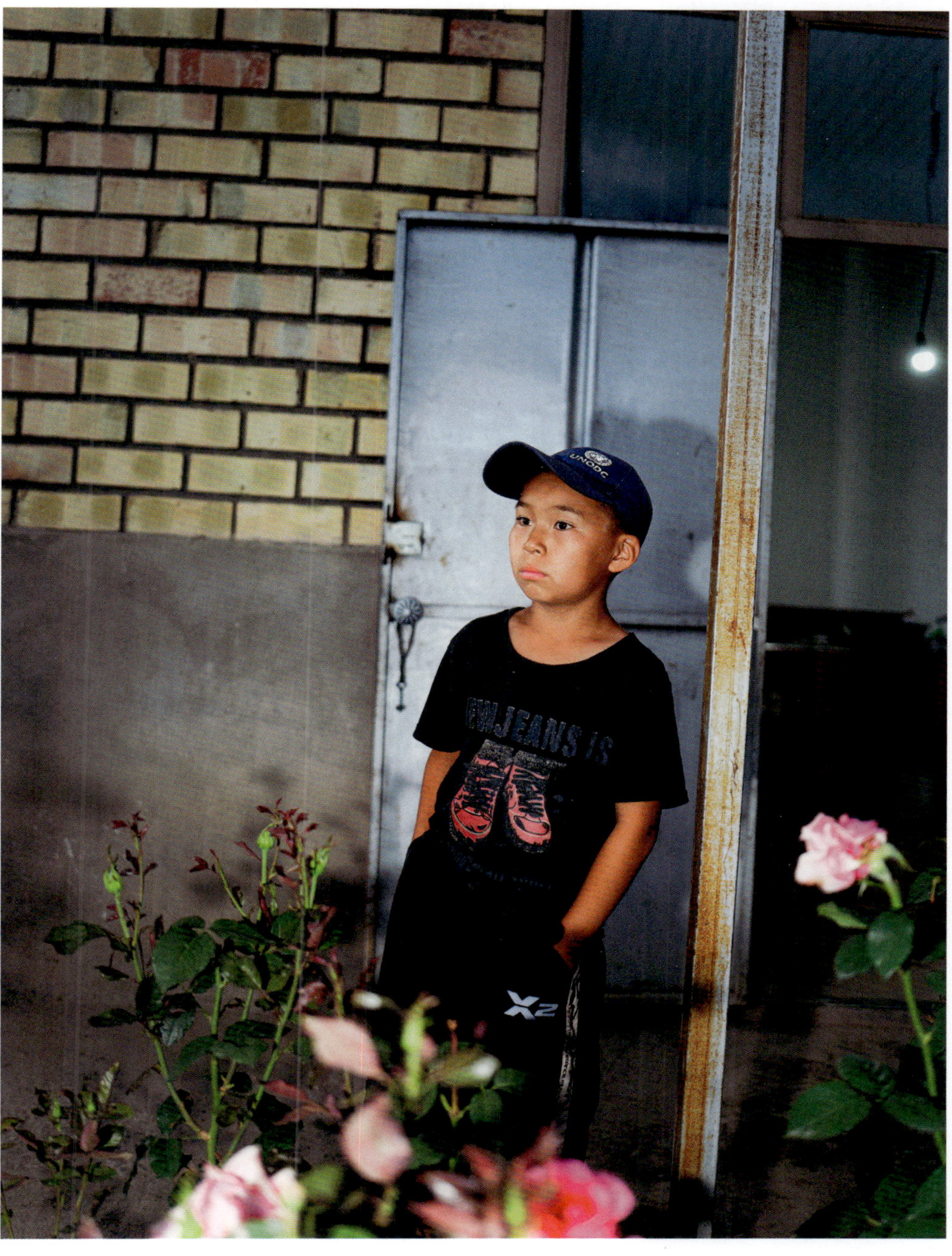

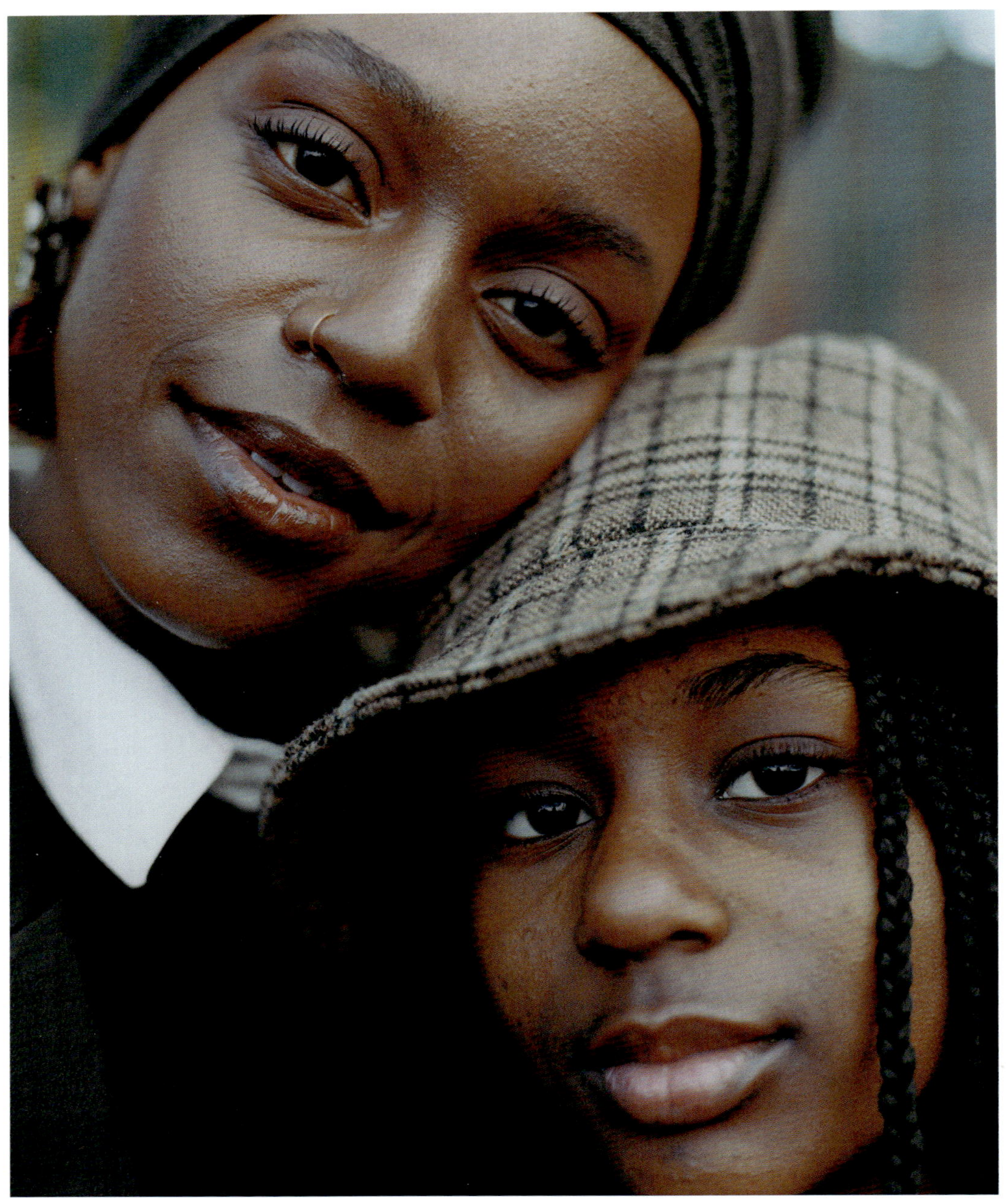

Garrod Kirkwood

Benedicta & Jasmine, September 2022
From the series *Siblings*
Chromogenic print

This portrait of sisters Benedicta and Jasmine forms part of British photographer Garrod Kirkwood's ongoing exploration of sibling relationships. A craving for human interaction, following COVID-19 restrictions, drove Kirkwood to make intimate and honest portraits. He approached his sitters after watching a documentary about their parents' migration to the UK from Africa. The two sisters, born in different continents, are captured in natural light, devoid of styling. They are deeply connected to each other, yet engaged with the viewer.

Jonangelo Molinari
Ncuti Gatwa, August 2022
Chromogenic print

London-based photographer Jonangelo Molinari made this portrait of the Rwandan-Scottish actor Ncuti Gatwa as he showed some of his favourite possessions for a video. These included items connected to his childhood, following his family fleeing the Rwandan genocide against the Tutsi minority and settling in Scotland. Praised for his Shakespearean work on stage, Gatwa came to prominence in the comedy-drama series *Sex Education* (2019–) and will be the next incarnation of the Doctor in *Doctor Who*.

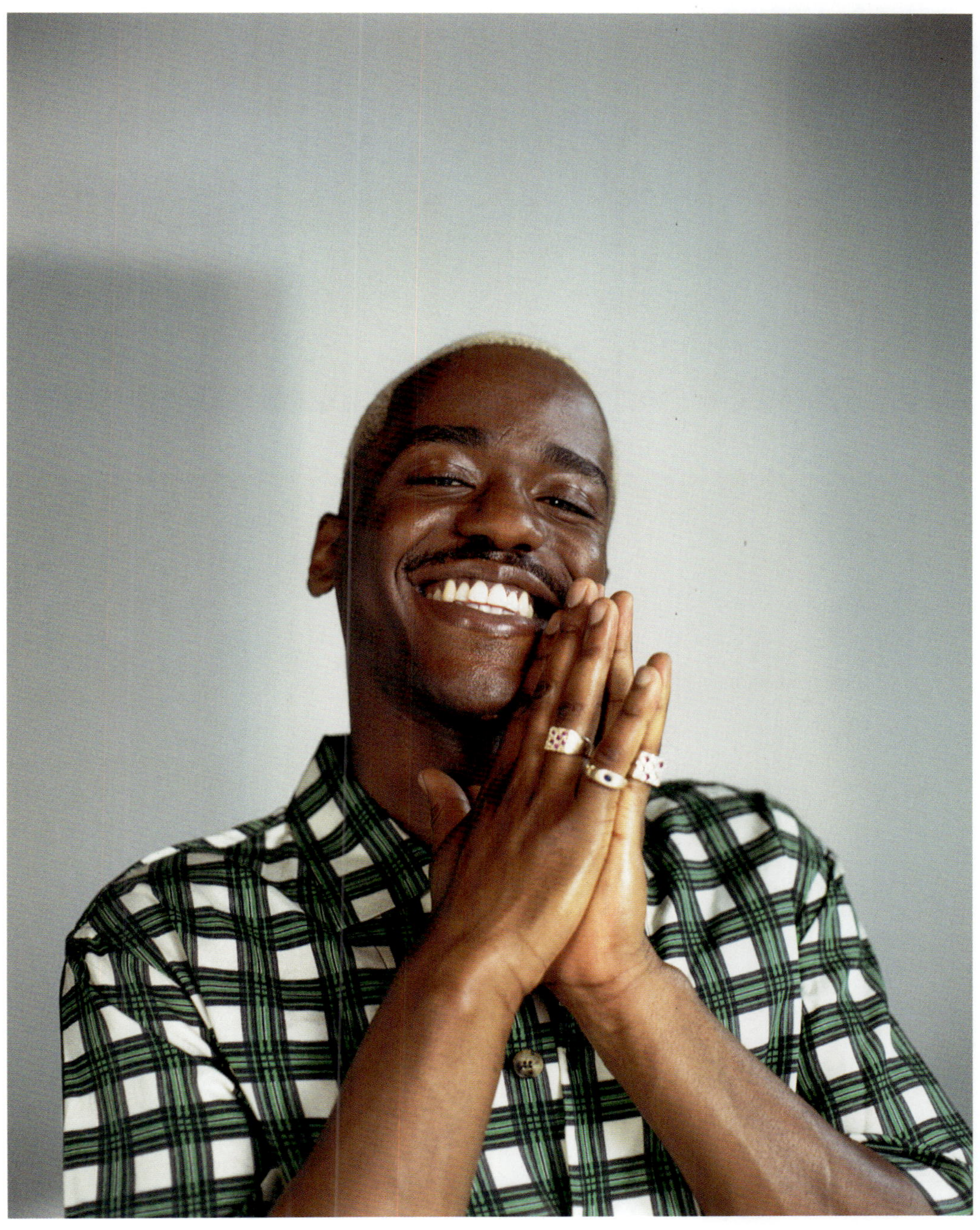

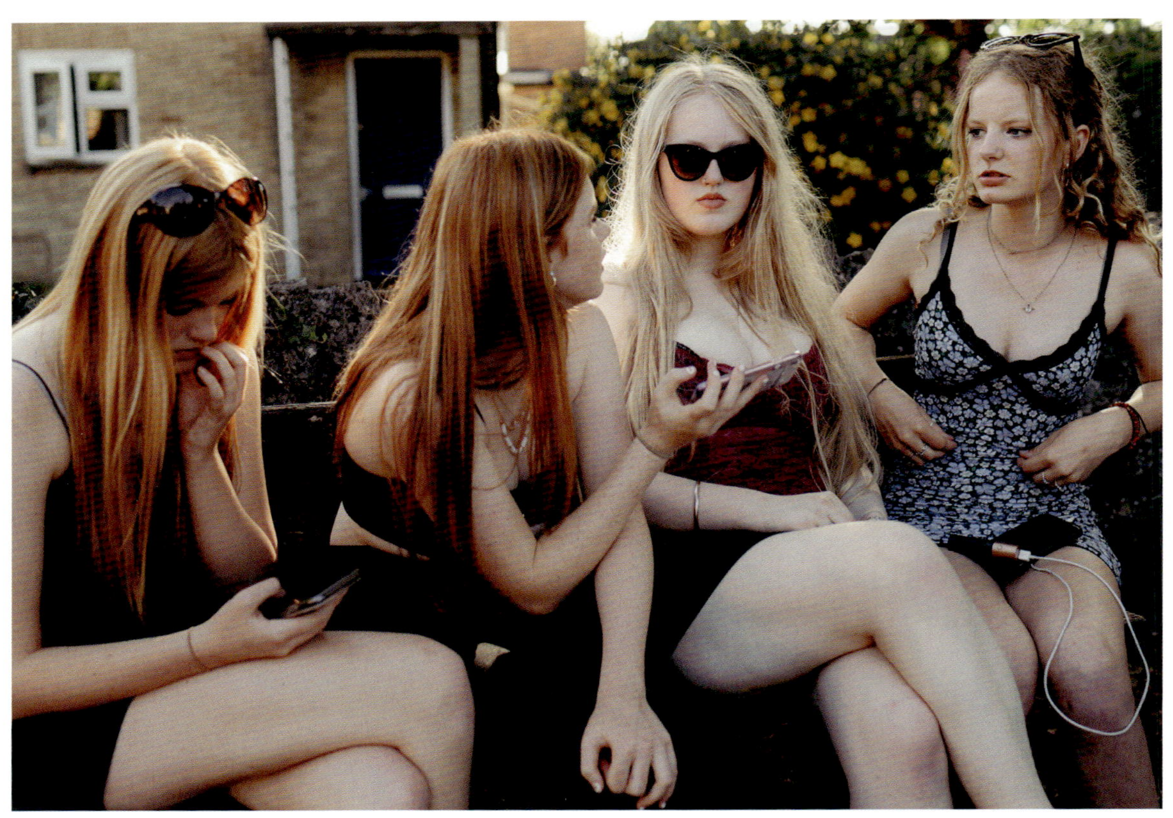

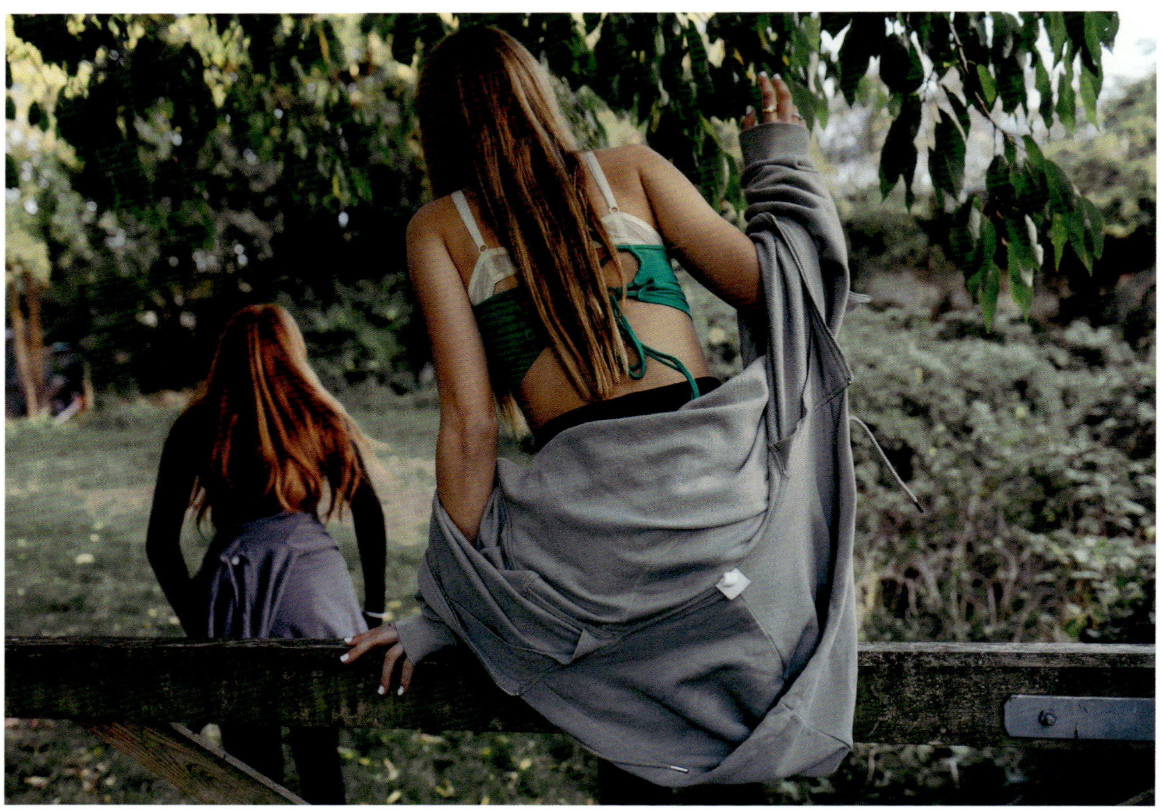

Philippa James
Scrolling, June 2022
Hidden Quarry, October 2022
TikTok, June 2022
From the series *No Big Deal*
Chromogenic prints

No Big Deal is a work-in-progress project featuring Philippa James's 14-year-old daughter and her friends, all born at the dawn of the smartphone era. The British photographer explains the intention of the series is to uncover the relationship teens have with their mobile phones: 'Surrounded by her friends making TikToks, I catch Lucy's eye as she strikes a pose that has perhaps been learned through social media. Since collaborating with the girls, we have had many discussions on sexual harassment, sexism and victim blaming. Misogyny can be hidden and invisible at times; I recognise this from when I was a teen girl.'

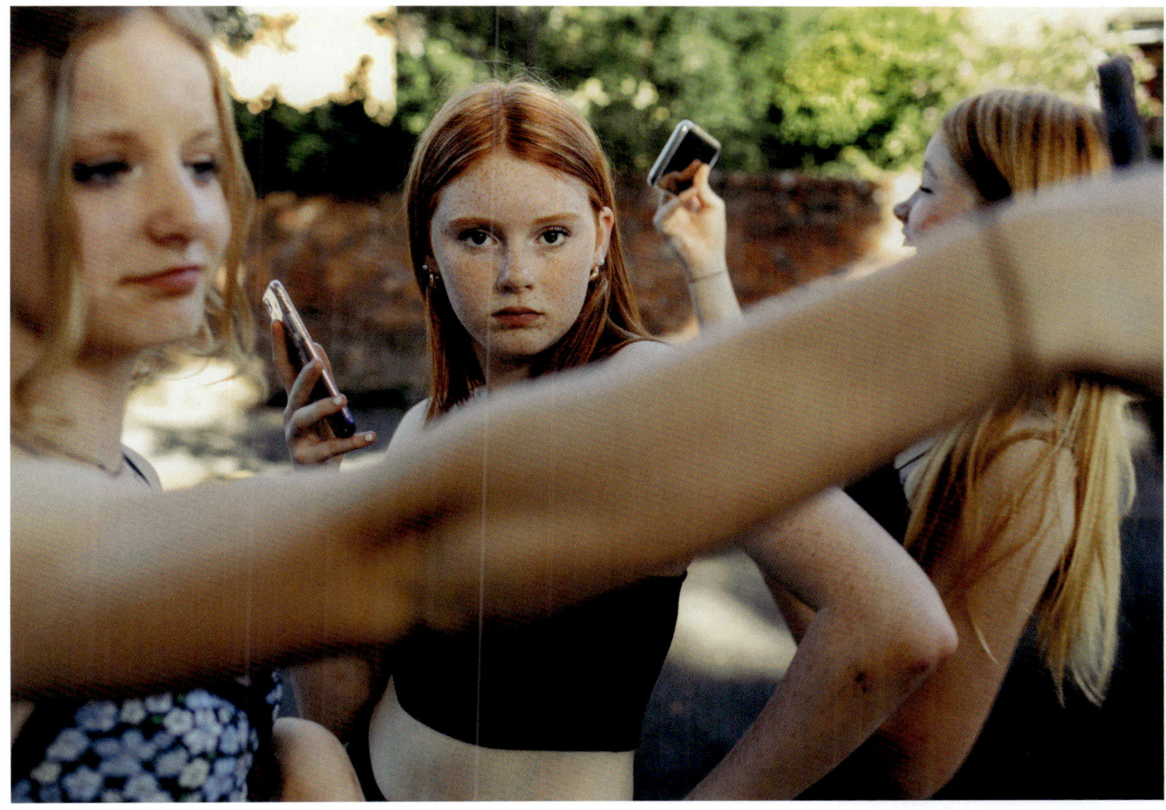

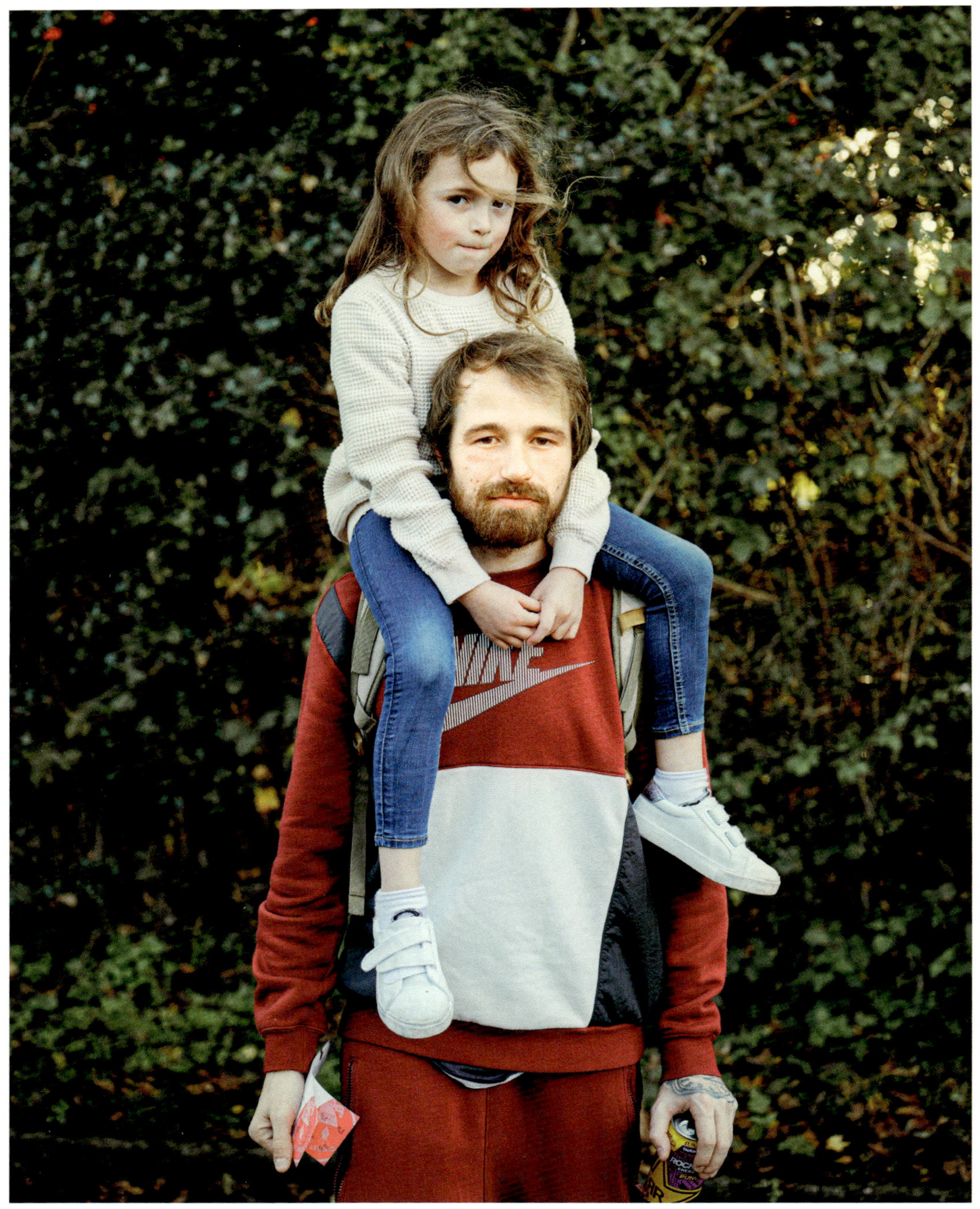

Kate Peters

Reece and his daughter, Crawley Town FC vs Barrow, November 2022
From the series *Crawley Town FC*
Chromogenic print

Commissioned by Jason Potterton and ESPN to photograph a story on Crawley Town Football Club after their takeover by cryptocurrency investors WAGMI United, London-based photographer Kate Peters focused on documenting fans of this fiercely traditional club who were wary of the takeover. Reece and his daughter Francesca were heading to the stadium to watch Crawley Town F.C. vs Barrow A.F.C. at home. Crawley won 1-0.

Enda Bowe

Dara watching the game, July 2022
From the series *Home on Thursdays*
Chromogenic print

After the death of his father, Irish photographer Enda Bowe realised how infrequently he had photographed his family. On regular Thursday night visits to his parent's home, he focused his lens on ordinary and cherished family moments previously missed. A portrait from this series shows his younger brother Dara in a Kilkenny county hurling shirt, absorbed in watching the All-Ireland semi-final. The sport of hurling holds special meaning to the family: Bowe's father played for Kilkenny, and as the photographer notes, 'he is there with Dara in the pictures on the shelves.'

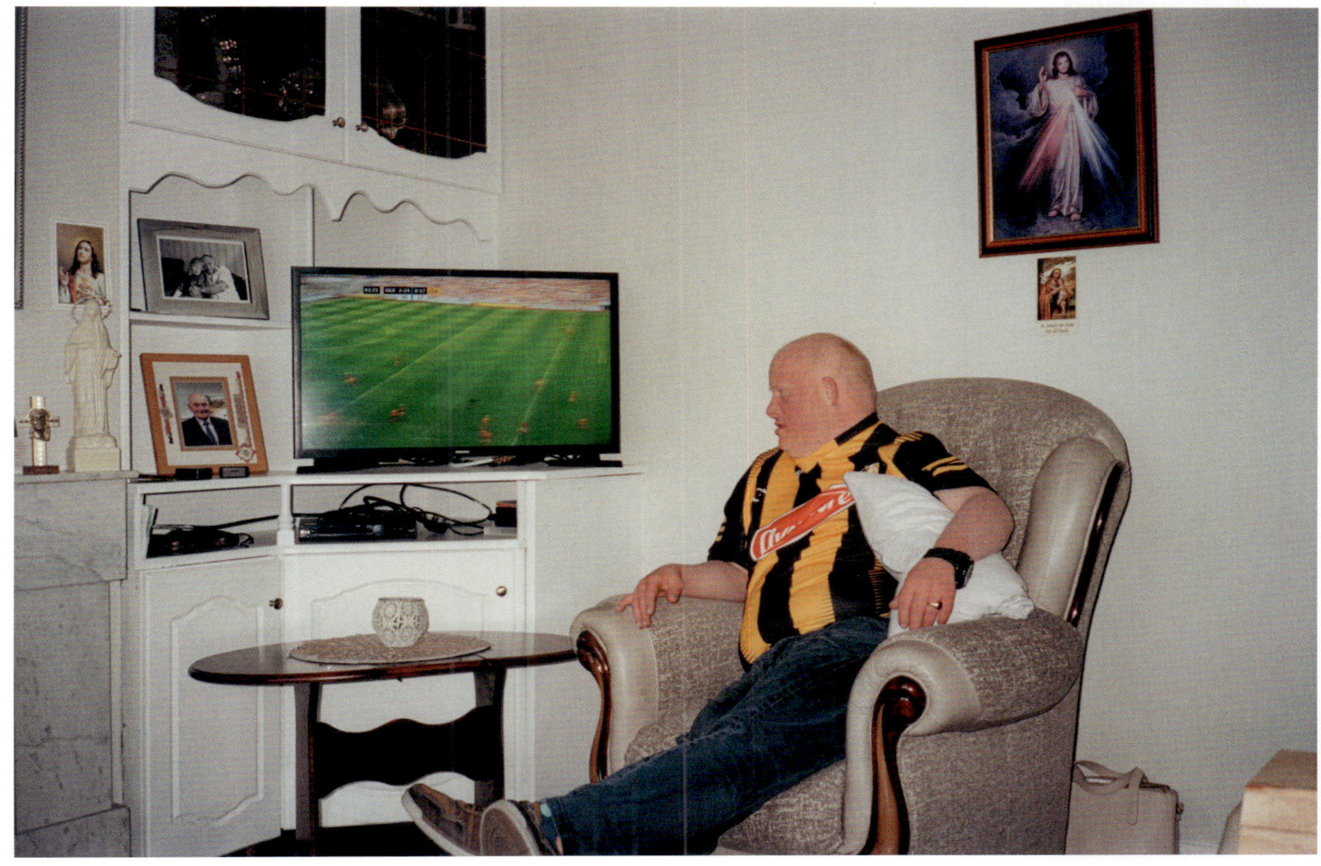

Tom Maguire

George, Malaita Province, Solomon Islands,
March 2023
Apollonia, Malaita Province, Solomon Islands,
March 2023
From the series *Rising Waters*
Inkjet prints

Tom Maguire's series focuses on children living in coastal communities affected by rising sea levels. The British picture editor and photographer met teenagers Apollonia and George in Malaita Province during a photo shoot with charity Save the Children, which aimed to highlight the experiences of a new generation living on the front line of the climate crisis in the Solomon Islands – one of the most vulnerable countries in the world to climate change and natural disasters.

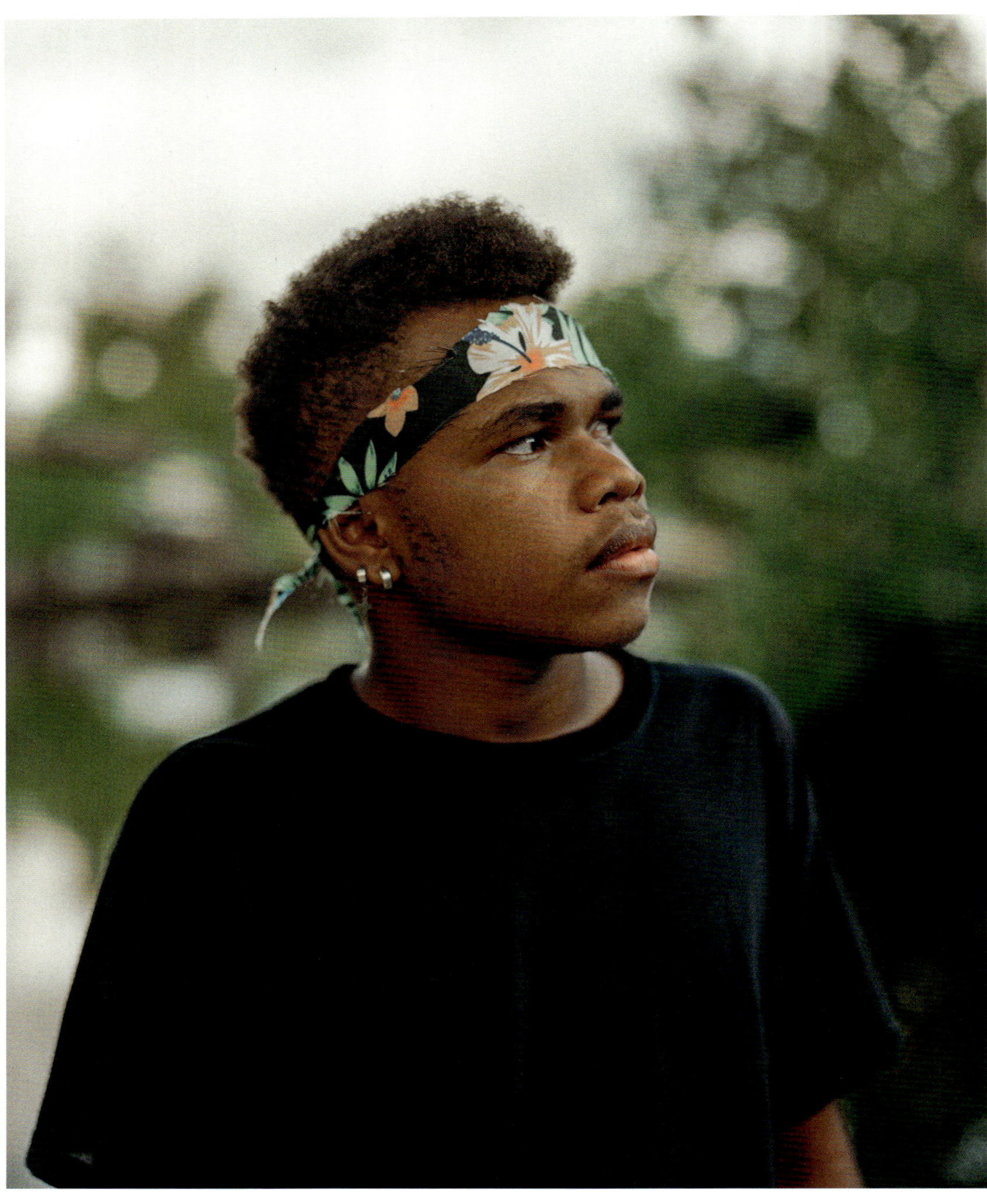

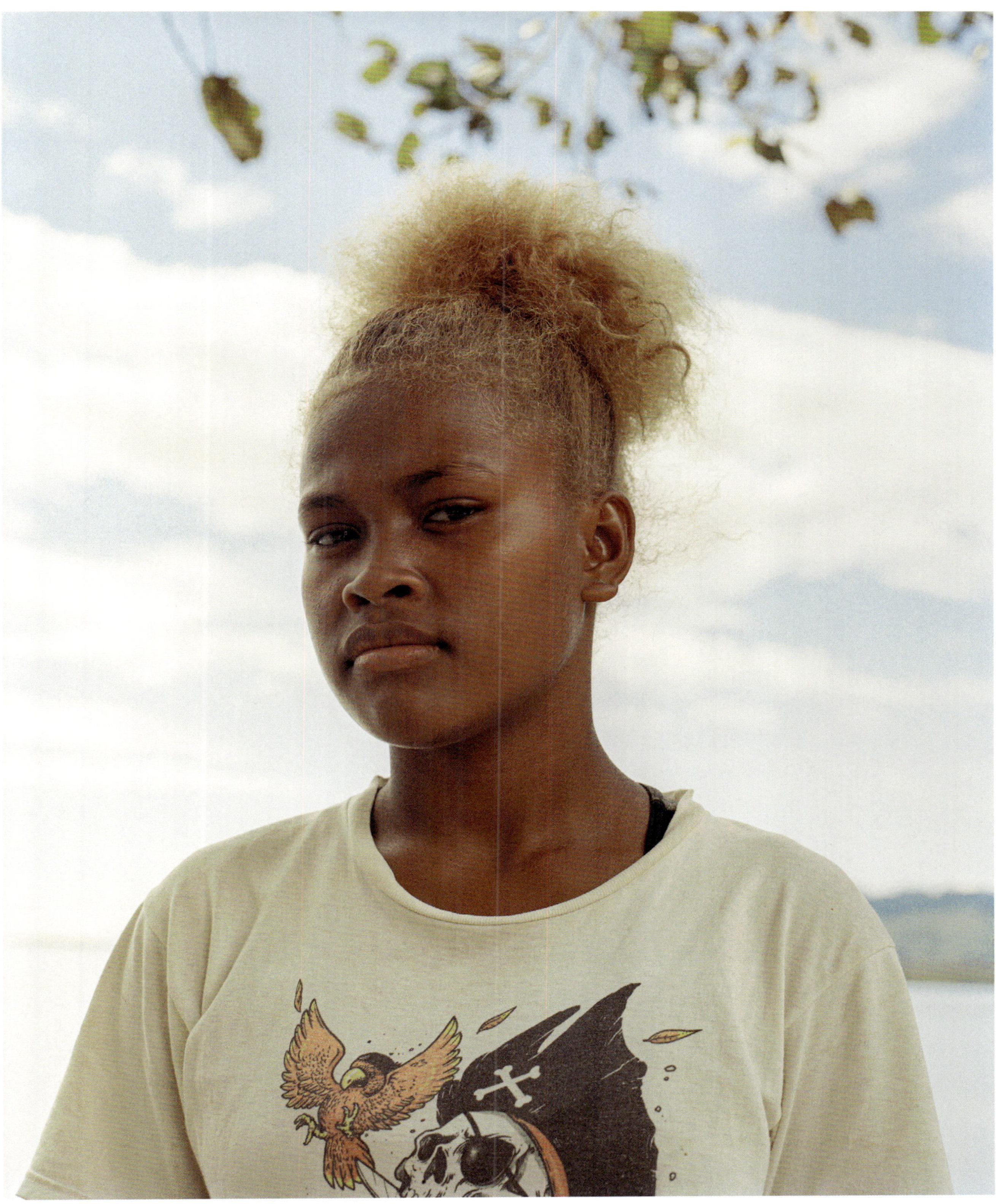

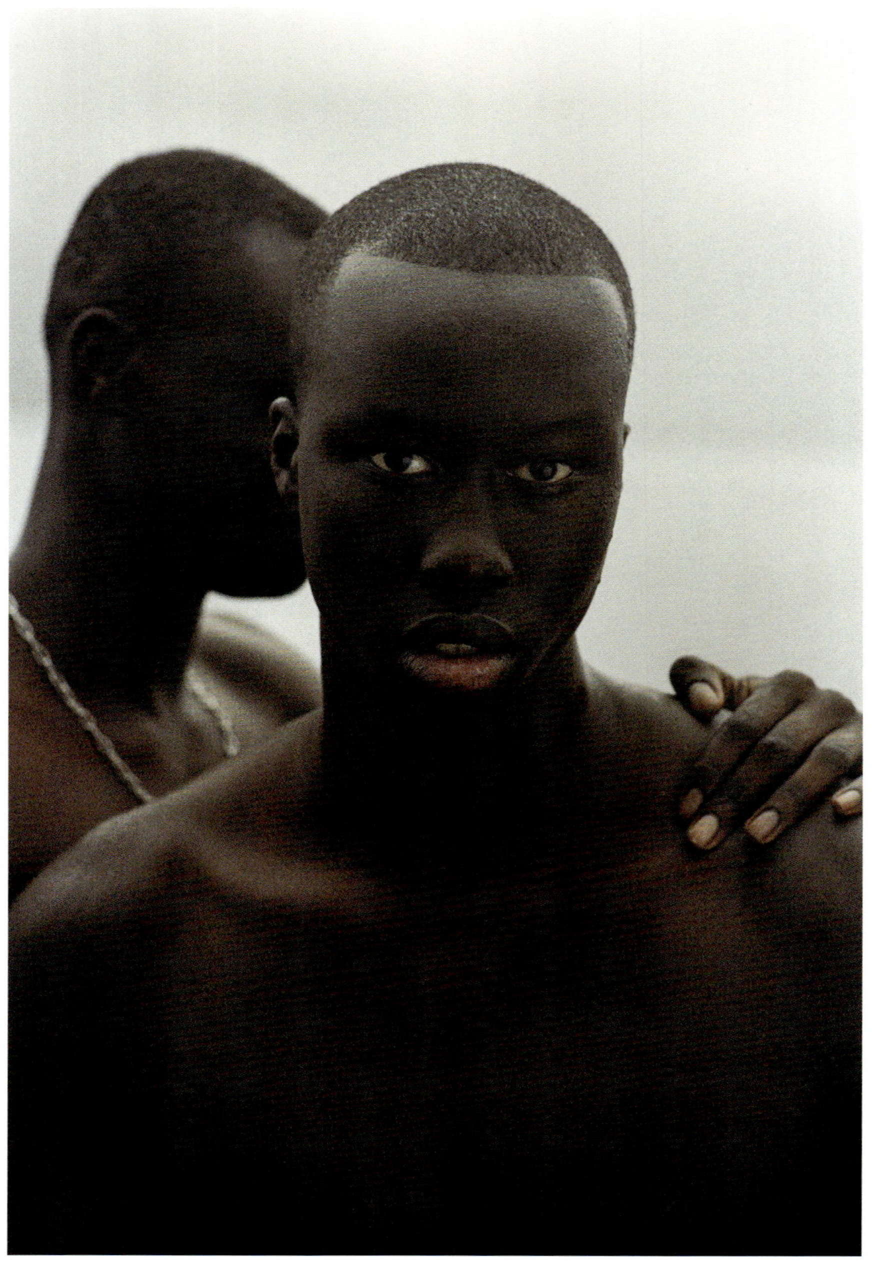

David van Dartel
Biliew & Paduey II, June 2022
From the series *What Once Was*
Chromogenic print

Dutch photographer David van Dartel's series explores friendship and masculinity through portraits of young adults in European countries. Brothers Biliew and Paduey fled Sudan at a young age, settling in Glasgow. They were photographed on a trip to Loch Lomond, the first time they had visited the Scottish Highlands. Van Dartel's portrait expresses the emotional intimacy, trust and vulnerability shared by the brothers, as a counterpoint to representations of masculine friendships traditionally centred on courage, power and heroism.

Rona Bar and Ofek Avshalom

Roy and Josef with their daughter Jude,
March 2022
From the series *Us*
Chromogenic print

Over two years, Israeli photographers Rona Bar and Ofek Avshalom photographed couples in their homes across Israel, the United Kingdom and Europe, drawing attention to families often overlooked by the mainstream media. Heavily tattooed couple Roy and Josef pose with their son Jude in Tel Aviv, updating the traditional motif of the Madonna and Child from art history. The close cropping of the portrait, together with a composition in which the contours of their individual bodies overlap, speaks to the family's close bond and connection.

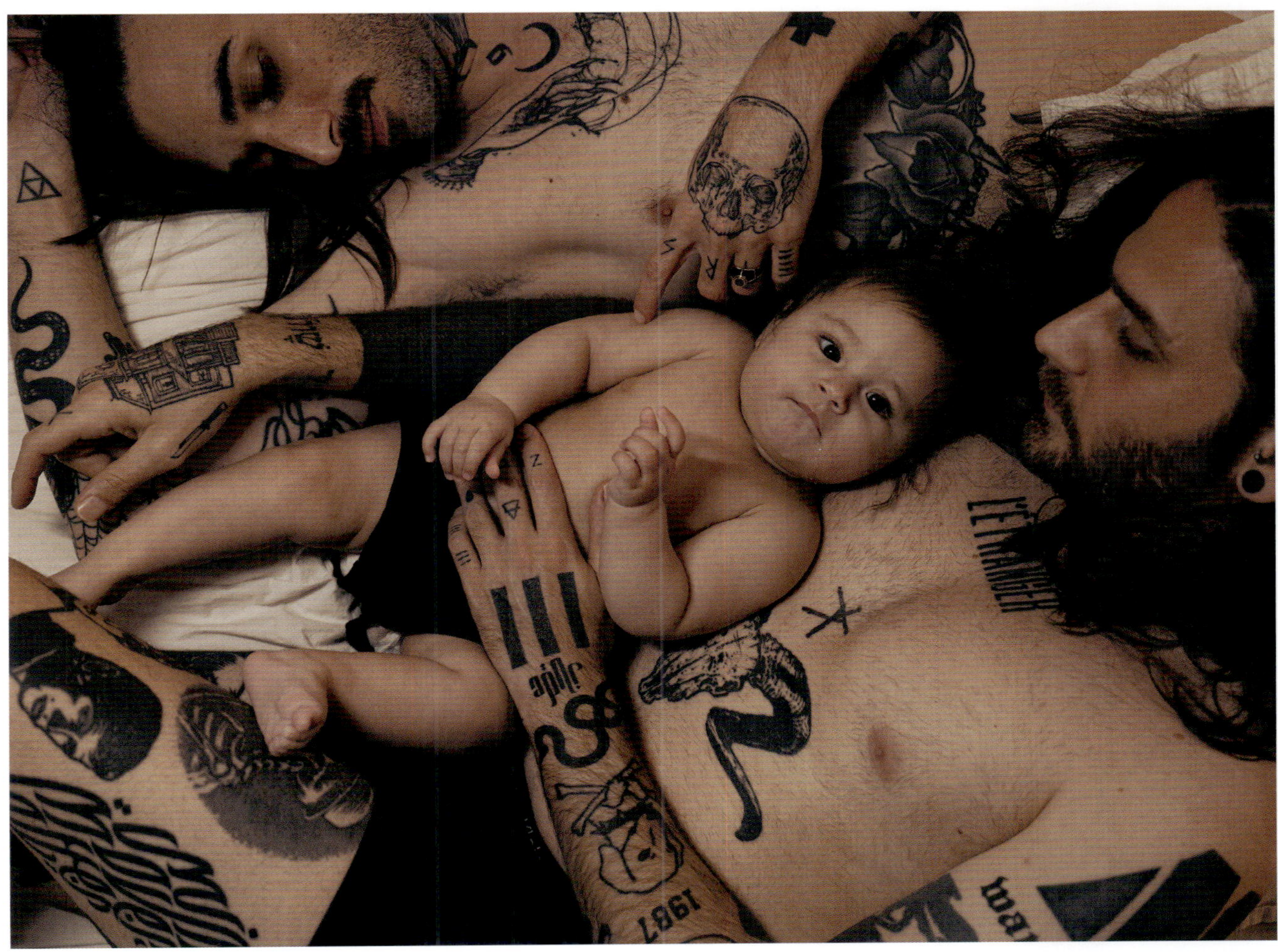

Michelle Sank

Zhara, Sea Point Pavilion, Cape Town,
March 2023
From the series *Ballade*
Chromogenic print

The series *Ballade* is a poetic homage to Michelle Sank's birthplace of Cape Town, which she left in 1978. Returning to South Africa in 2022, the photographer was drawn to revisit the spaces of her youth, including Sea Point Promenade and its accompanying swimming pool, which she describes as 'stage sets within which diverse performances unfolded.' Sank was taken by Zhara's statuesque presence by the pool, her clothes emblazoned with the inclusive message 'Love More.'

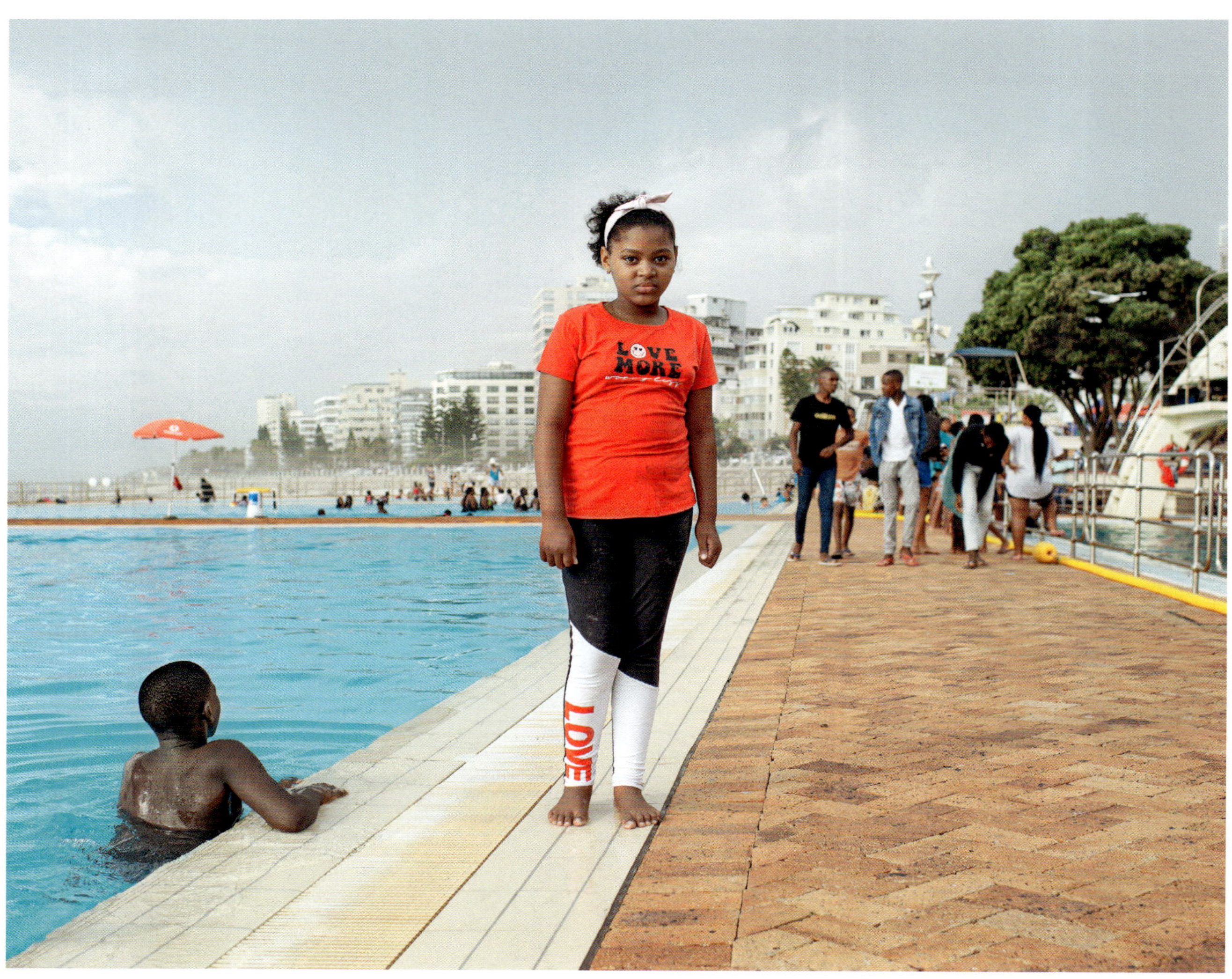

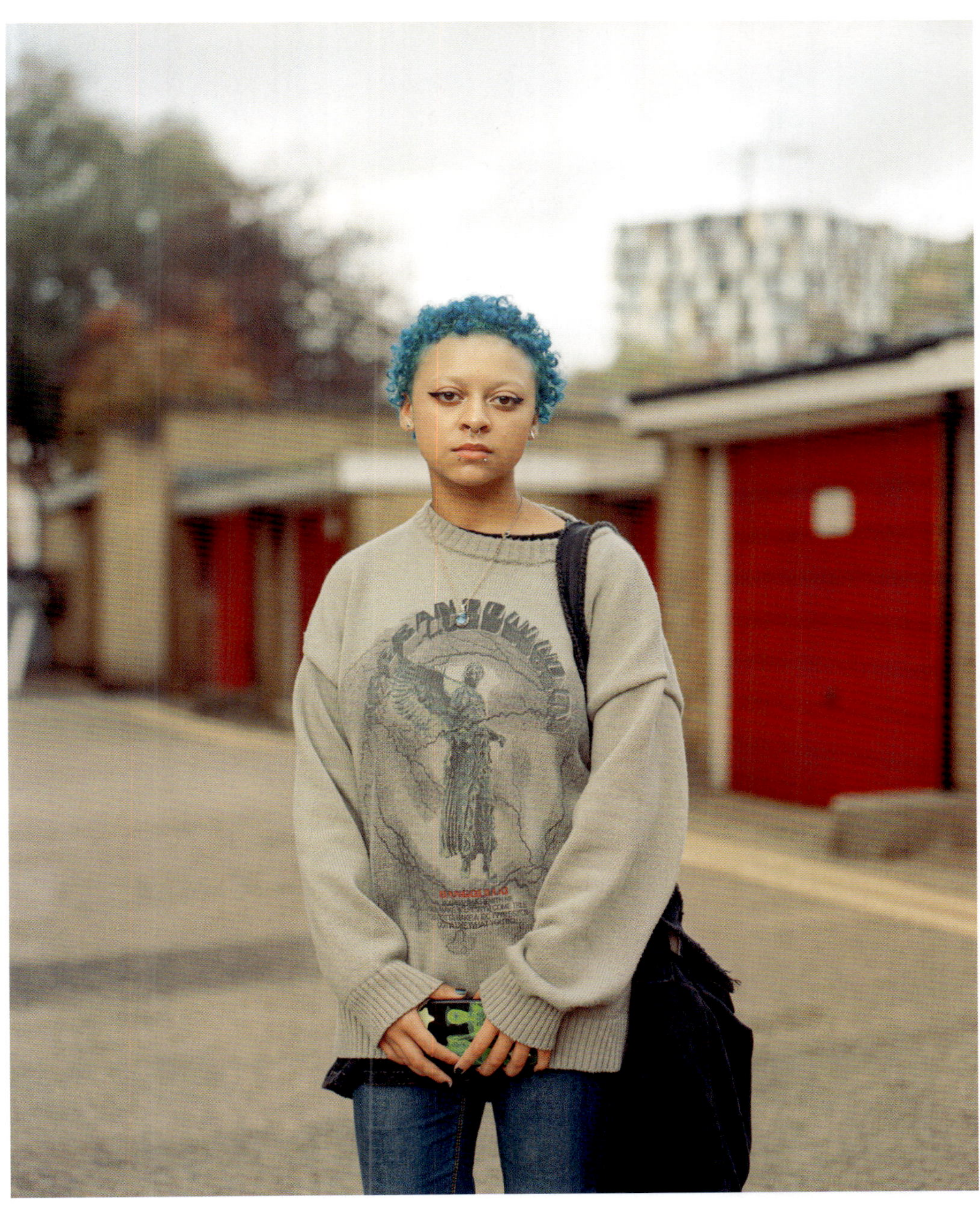

Freya Najade

Kiera, October 2022
From the series *Hackney Central*
Inkjet print

When German photographer Freya Najade moved to London 15 years ago, she fell in love with Hackney, one of the most diverse boroughs in London where more than 89 languages are spoken. Najade set out to capture the energy of the area, marked by 'peaceful coexistence of many ways of being – different cultures, languages, ethnic groups and social and economic classes.' Centring her project on Hackney Central railway station, she chanced upon Kiera nearby, her blue hair and matching jewellery standing out against the red garage doors.

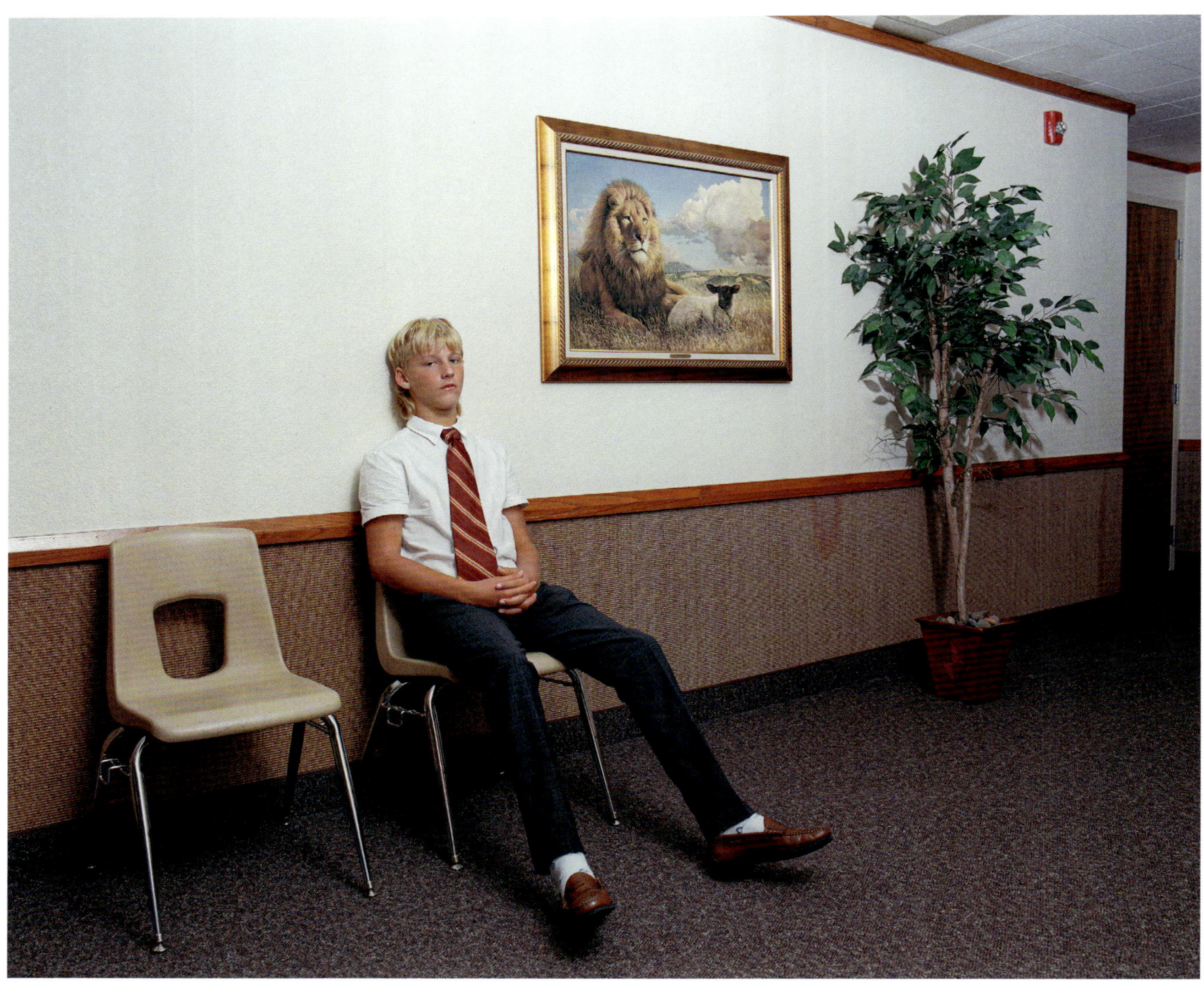

Fumi Nagasaka

Andrew, September 2022
Chromogenic print

Since 2002, Japanese photographer Fumi Nagasaka has been based in New York and exploring American youth culture through photography. She met Andrew at the Church of Jesus Christ of Latter-day Saints in Southlake, Texas, while working on a wider documentary about young people in the church. Nagasaka captured Andrew seated in a moment of repose from serving water and crackers to the congregation, and wryly noted the way his hair bore a striking resemblance to the lion's mane in the picture beside him.

Roo Lewis

Captain Beany, February 2022
From the series *Port Talbot UFO Investigation Club*
Chromogenic print

In 1991, Barry Kirk legally changed his name to his superhero persona, Captain Beany, and established the world's only baked bean museum from his council flat in Sandfields, Port Talbot, which sits just off the M4 motorway in South Wales. Once dominated by the steel industry, the town has produced iconic actors including Richard Burton, Anthony Hopkins and Michael Sheen, and is also the site of unusually high numbers of UFO sightings. London-based photographer Roo Lewis used these phenomena as a starting point for a photographic project that explores the people, landscapes and folklore of this small industrial town.

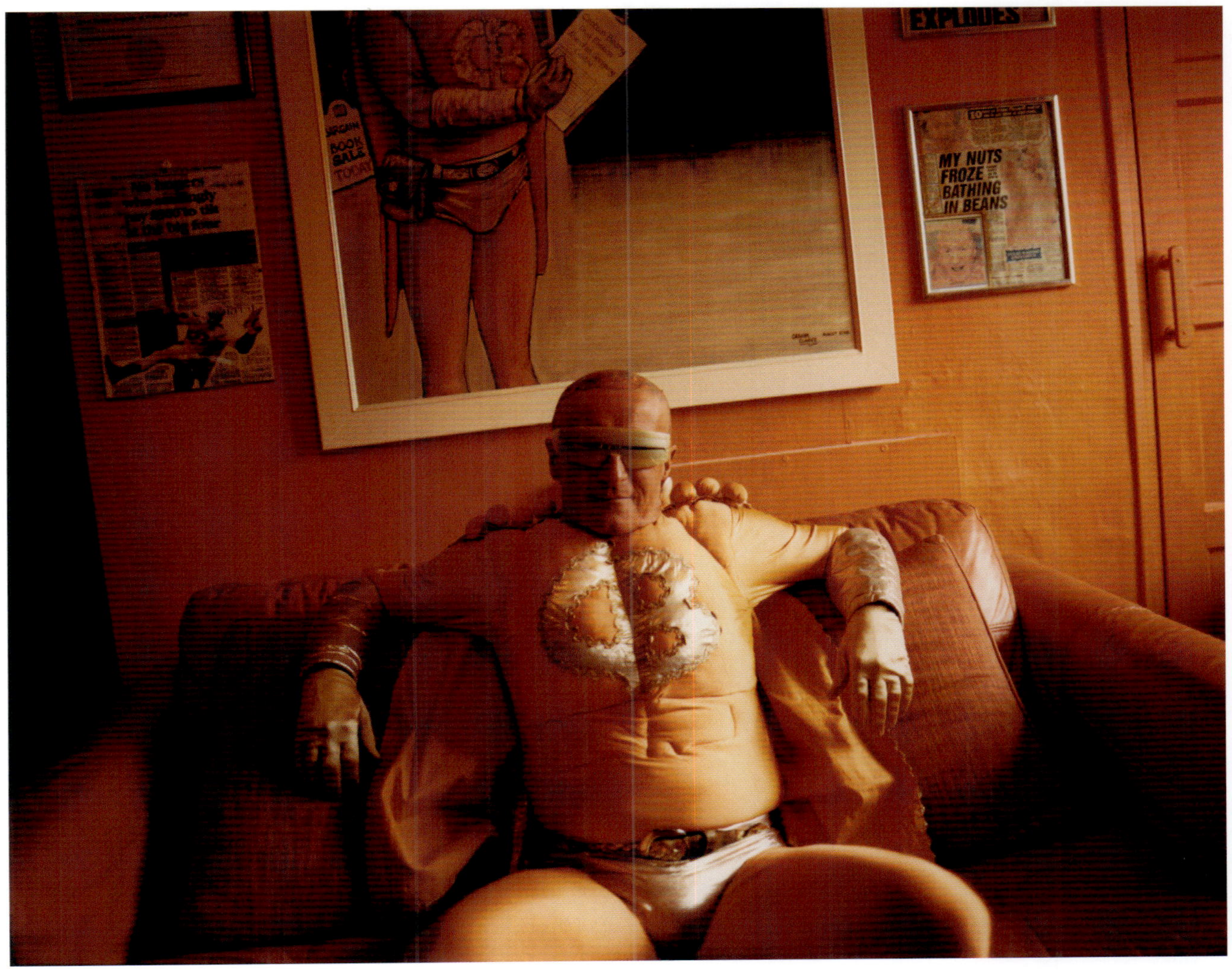

Louise Haywood-Schiefer
Kwajo Tweneboa, February 2023
Chromogenic print

British activist Kwajo Tweneboa used social media to challenge the nation's most powerful social housing companies. Following the death of his father in 2020, and having shared a vermin-infested flat with his family on the Eastfields Estate in Mitcham, Tweneboa exposed negligent conditions in private and social housing rentals, and revealed the ineffectiveness of the complaints system. This portrait by London-based photographer Louise Haywood-Schiefer was commissioned to accompany an interview with Tweneboa in *The House* magazine, a publication for MPs and peers.

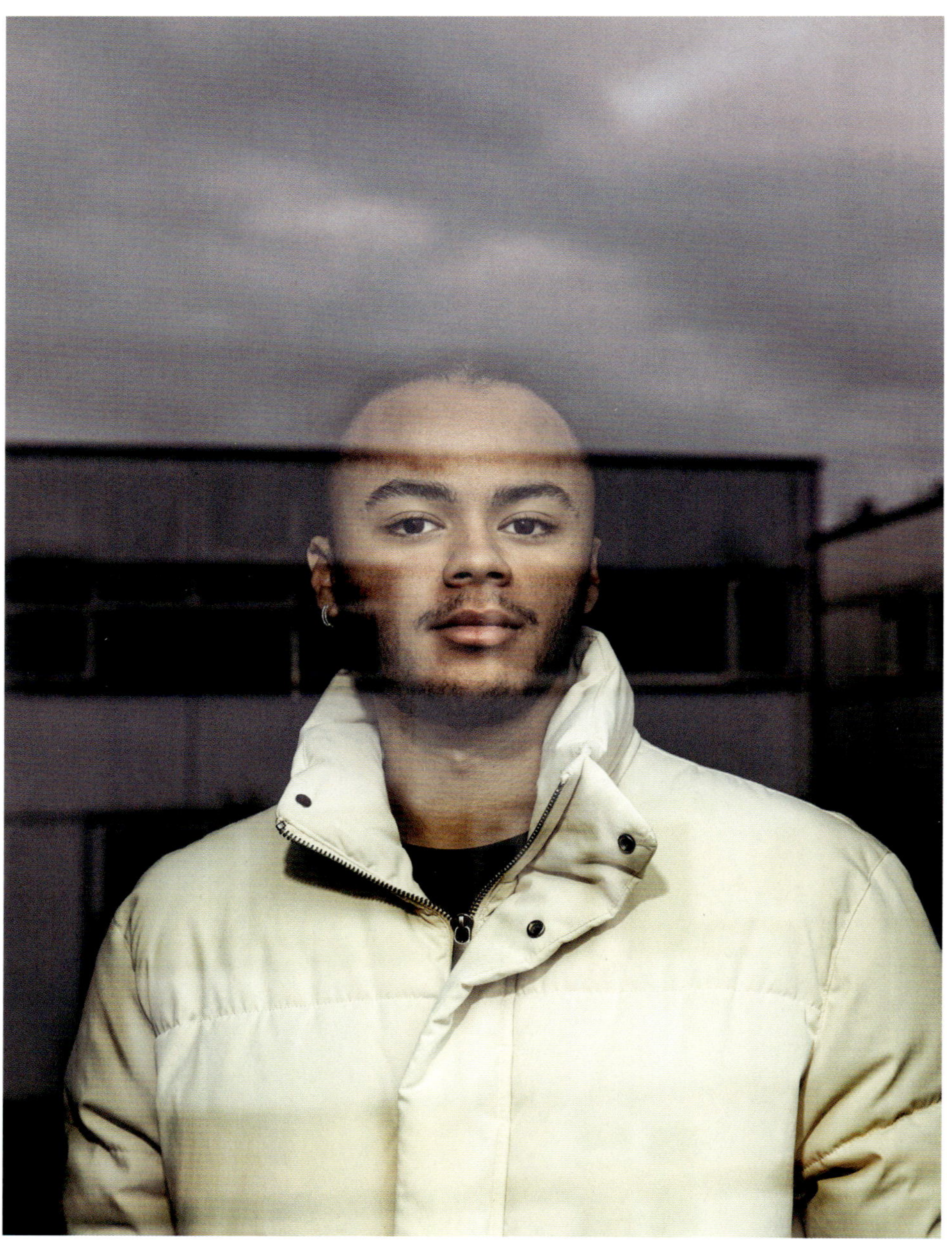

Daniel Kirmatzis
André, May 2022
Chromogenic print

Operations manager Daniel Kirmatzis takes portraits in his spare time, looking for people whose individuality rises above the crowd. He explains, 'to be oneself and to express individuality is the ultimate quest against the rise of standardised thinking, especially in a globalised world in which social media algorithms can force people to conform to how they should act, dress and think.' Having first photographed André in Piccadilly in 2019, he encountered his sitter again in 2022 at Photo London, a photographic fair held at Somerset House, where this portrait was taken.

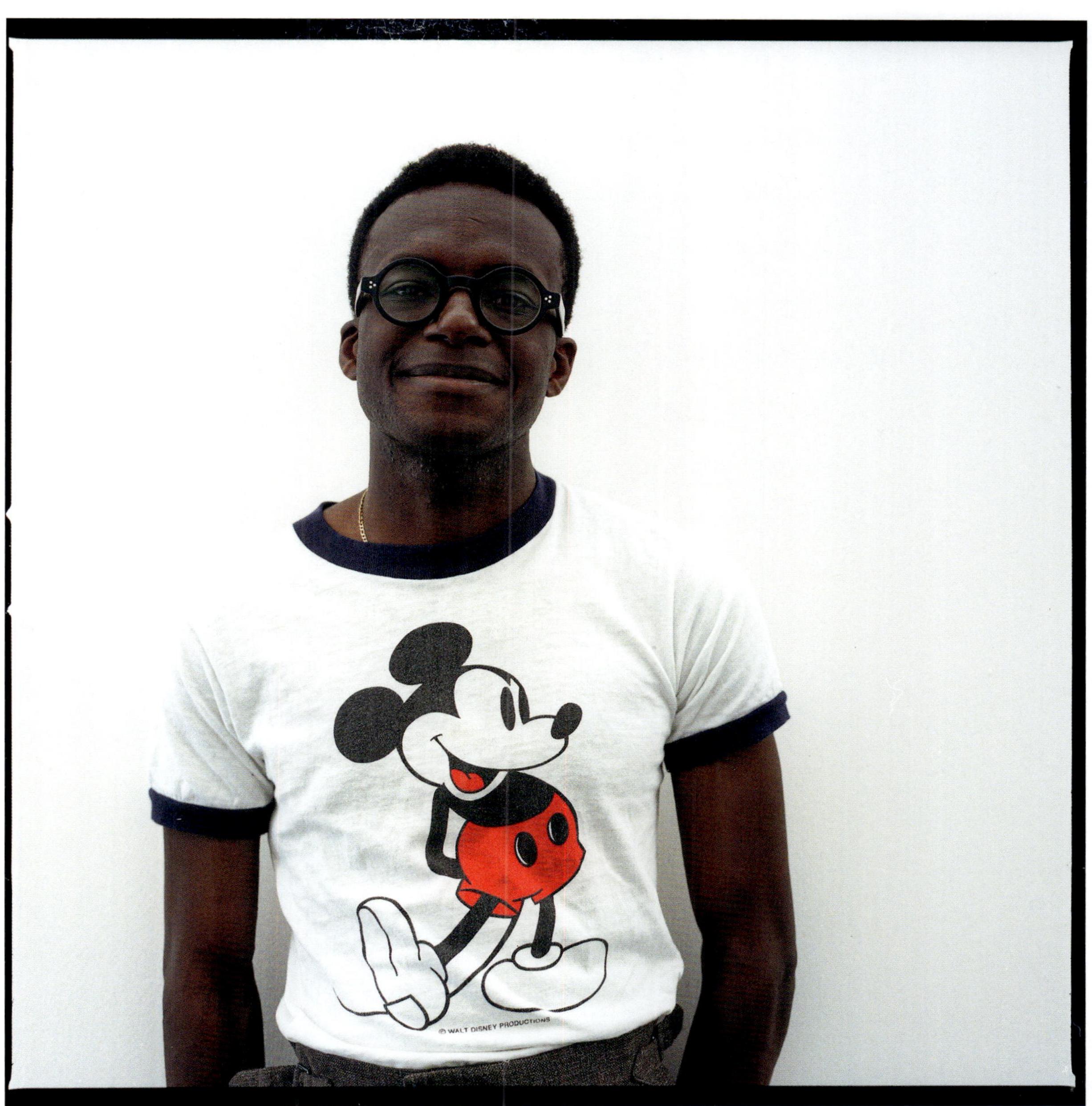

Zoja Kalinovskis
Phopy, December 2022
From the series *Unseen*
Inkjet print

As a disabled, queer, non-binary artist, Zoja Kalinovskis explains, 'I know what it's like to feel unseen.' The British photographer began the ongoing series *Unseen* 'to challenge the narrative around how disabled people are viewed, confronting the ableism that permeates our society and flipping the script on what disability "looks like" by intentionally including those with invisible disabilities.' This portrait shows their friend Phopy adopting a pose inspired by classical sculpture.

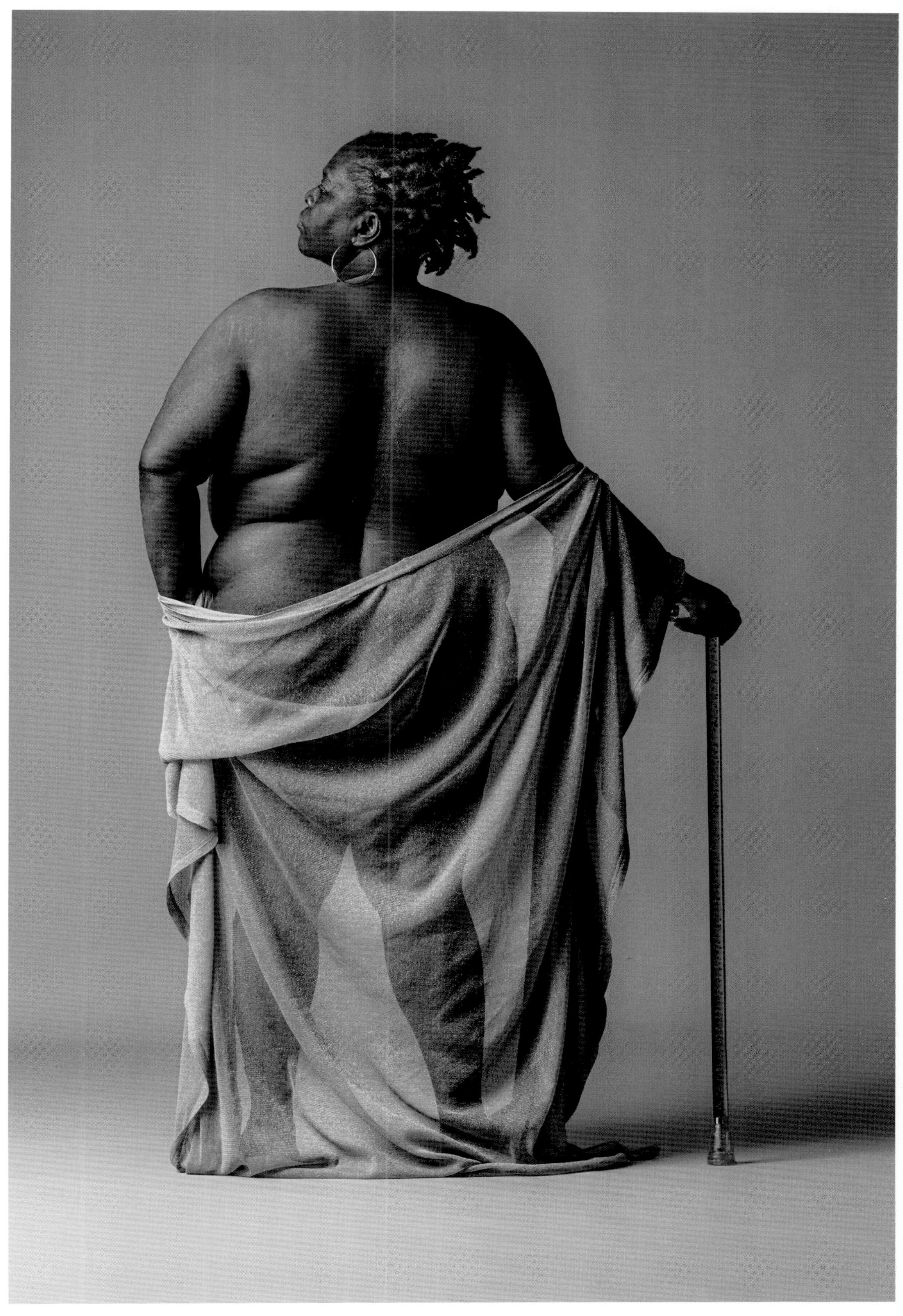

Theodore Clarke

*Abraham, aboard the MV Ilala, Lake Malawi,
between Mlowe and Usisya*, May 2023
From the series *The Boat On The Lake*
Inkjet print

The MV *Ilala* – a ferry built in Glasgow in 1949 – has
been sailing Lake Malawi since 1951. Predating Malawian
independence by 13 years, it is a unique remnant of
British colonialism. Irish-born photographer Theodore
Clarke was on deck at dawn when he encountered
Abraham wrapped in a pale blanket. Abraham, who
dreams of being a doctor, earns a living by fishing
with his uncle. Overfishing has made life hard for many
around the lake who rely on the water for their livelihoods.

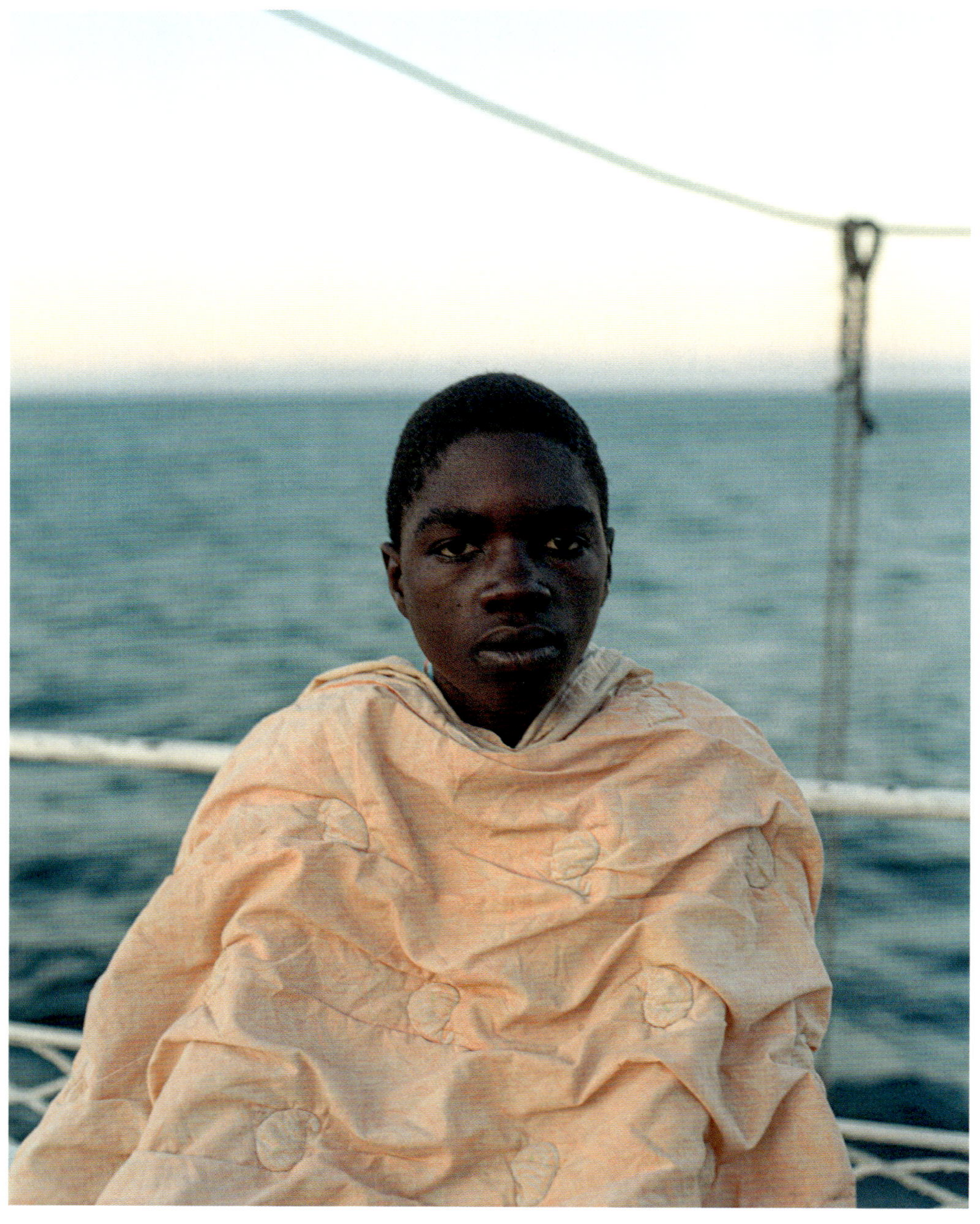

Gregory John Turner

Untitled, November 2022
From the series *Yesterday, and Today
and Forever*
Chromogenic print

Hannah, who is in recovery from heroin dependency,
has been suffering from addiction for the last 20 years.
Photographed on West Wittering beach in West Sussex,
she is in the process of building a new life for herself.
As part of this commitment, she has collaborated
with British portrait photographer Gregory John Turner
to share her story and create a visual record of her
experience. Turner remarked on 'the raw honesty' of
Hannah's engagement with the project: 'not once has
she flinched from disclosing challenging memories.'

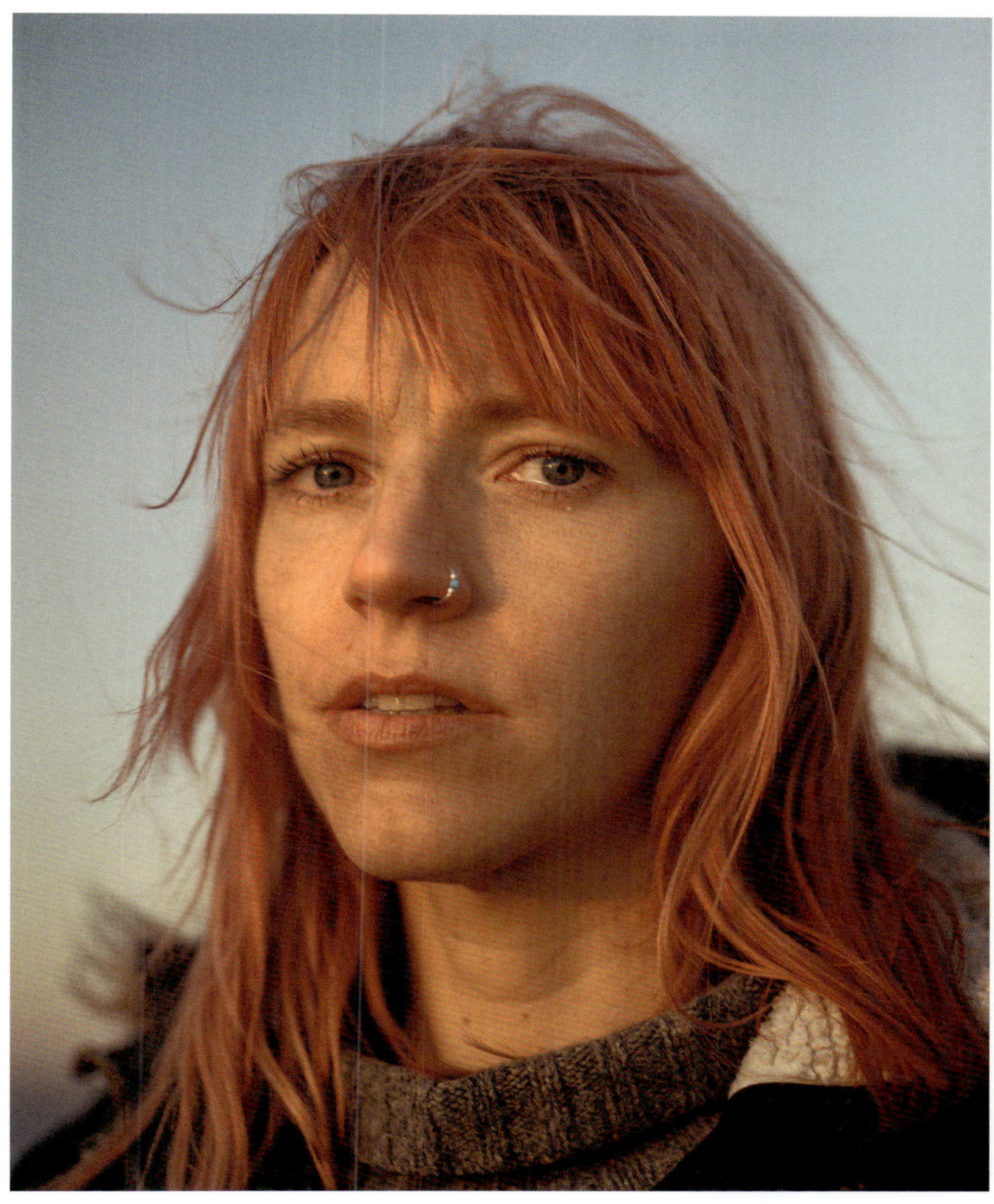

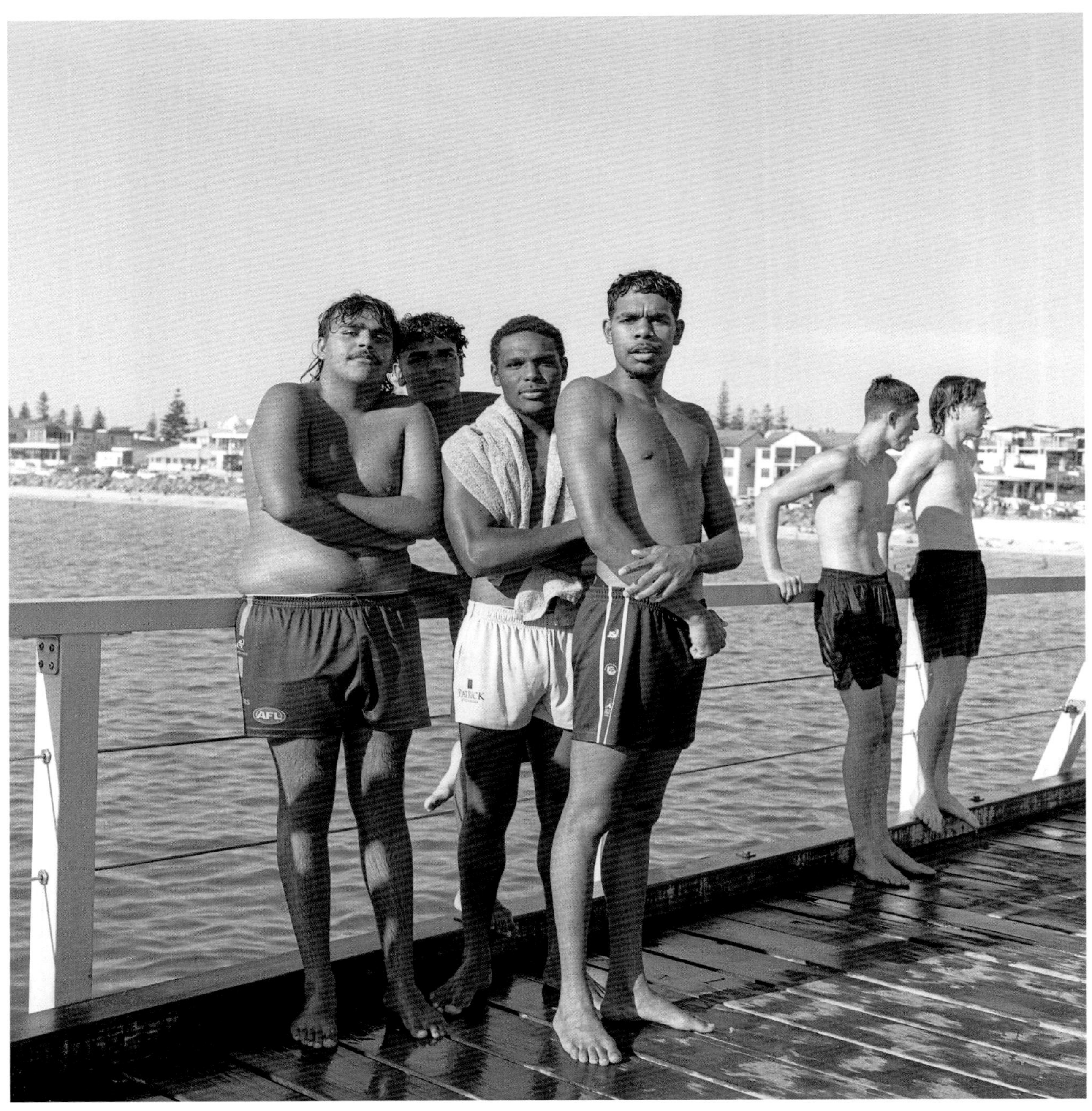

Alex Frayne

Halcyon Days, March 2023
From the series *Jetty Life*
Inkjet print

Australian photographer Alex Frayne has been photographing metropolitan jetties in his home town of Adelaide, South Australia, for a decade. He is 'fascinated by the intricate social relationships that exist between the youth groups who jump, laugh, flirt and revel' on these outdoor stages for male competitiveness and performance. Here, a group of young men present themselves with self-assuredness; Frayne recalled they were 'bathed in sun and fearless towards my probing camera.'

Margarita Galandina

Self-portrait with my brother, October 2022
From the series *Ovoo*
Inkjet print

London-based multidisciplinary artist Margarita Galandina grew up in the Republic of Buryatia, in south-central Siberia, and remains closely connected with her homeland. Pictured with her brother George, the self-portrait restages the earliest visual record she could find of her ancestors – a 1936 photograph of her great-grandmother, the last woman in her family to speak the indigenous Siberian language. Her series draws on oral histories, and explores her familial photographic archive, to reflect upon the family's complex history and heritage.

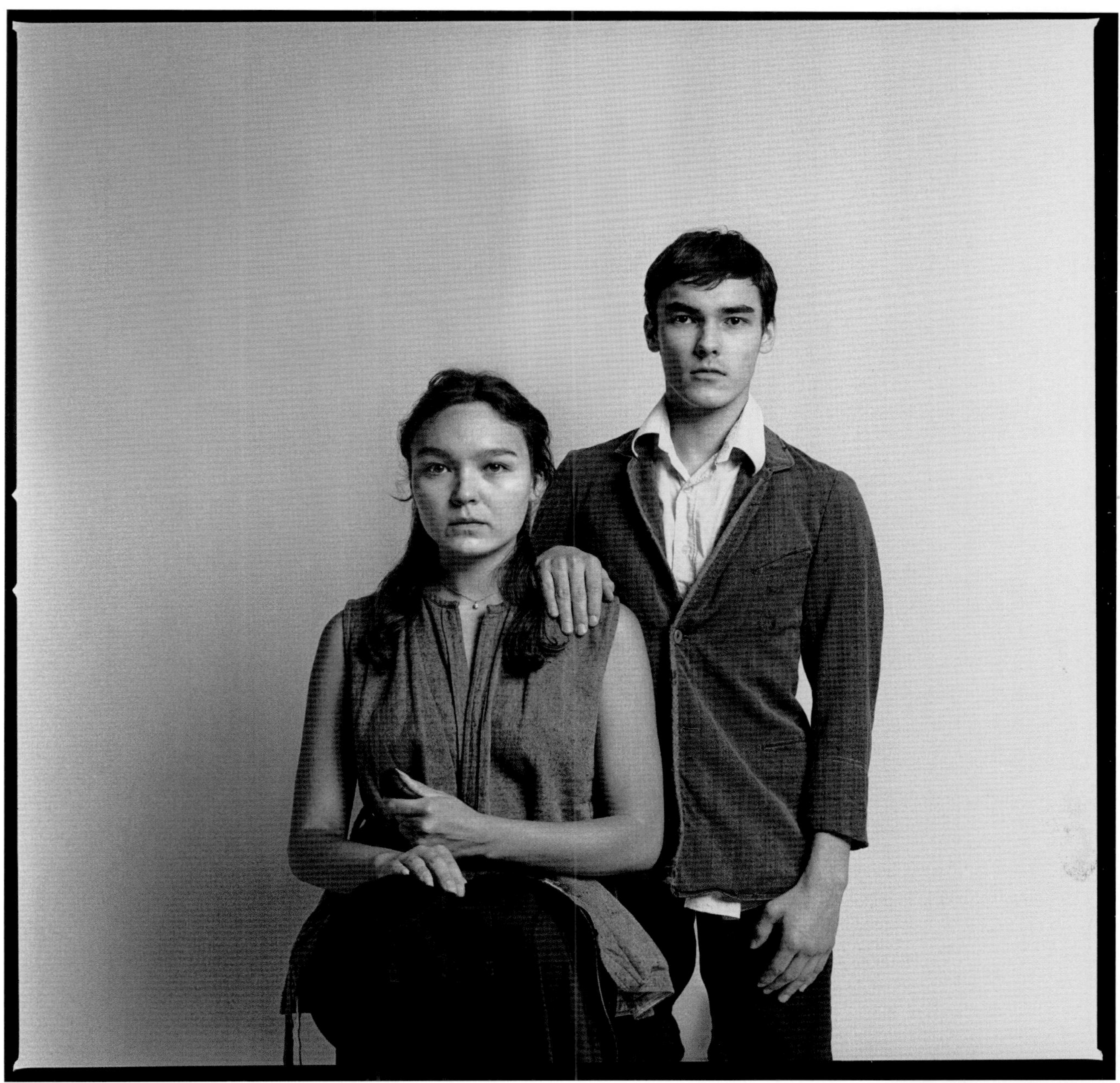

Lucas Troadec

*Mrs. Aldred in blue, with directions to the
bluebell flower fields on a spring day*, May 2022
From the series *End of the Line*
Inkjet print

French filmmaker and photographer Lucas Troadec
encountered Mrs Aldred while out cycling in Kennington,
south London. Compelled to take her portrait, it was the
first time Troadec had photographed a stranger, almost
three years after picking up a camera. He recalled, 'she
agreed to sit for me with a smile, and gave me directions
to a field of bluebell flowers nearby.' The portrait marked
the start of a project to explore the people and urban
landscapes of his new home in London.

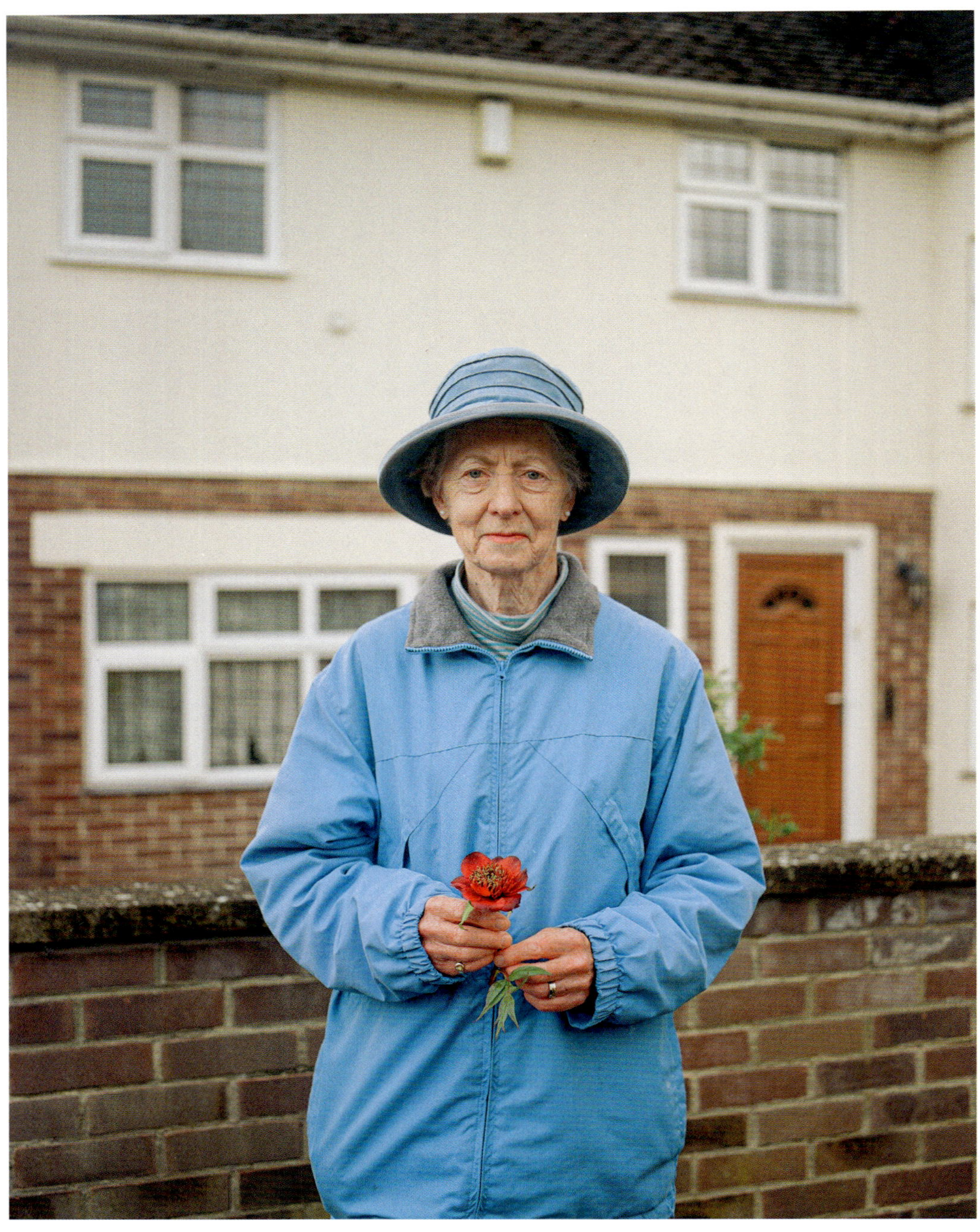

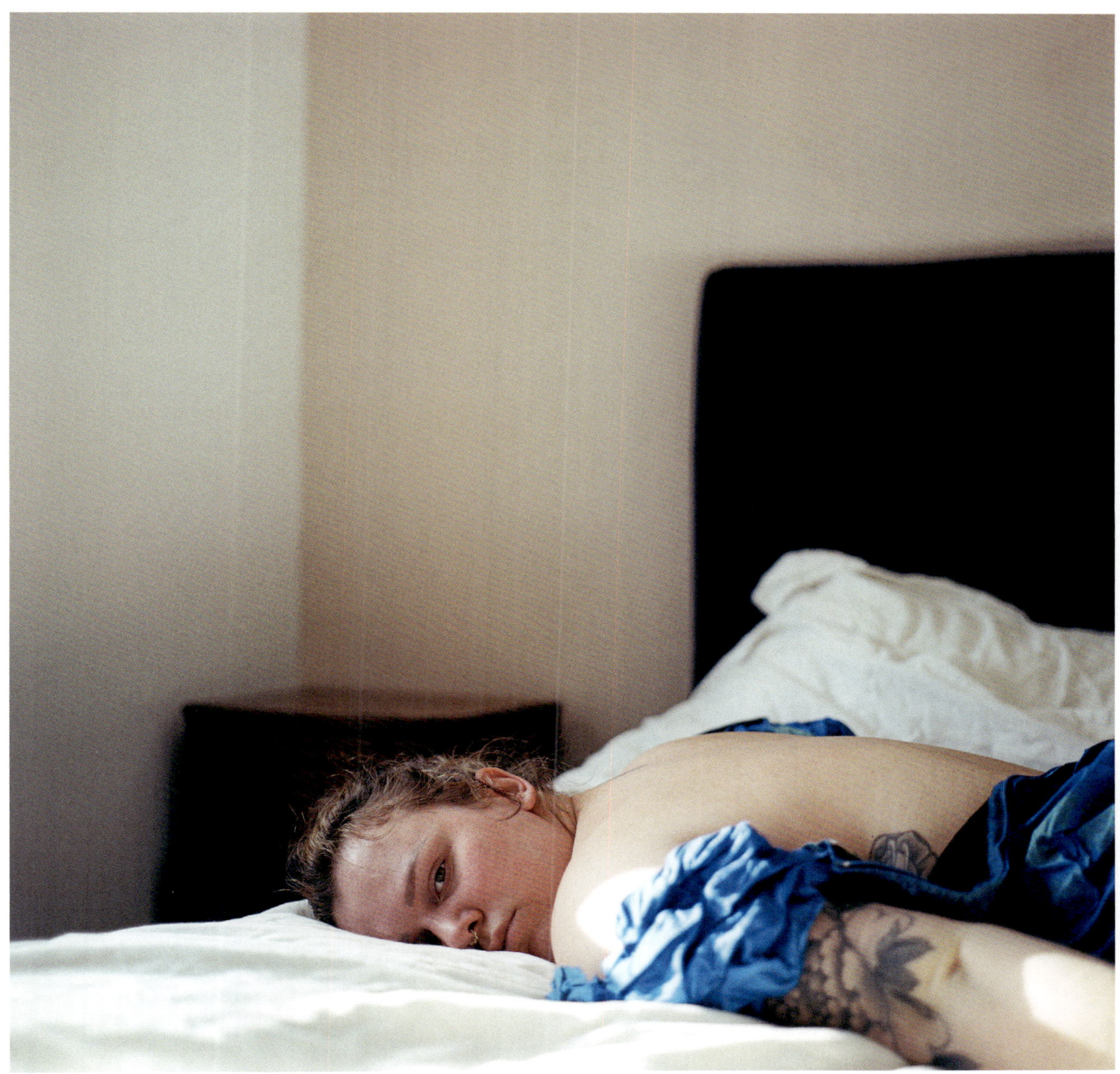

Cara Price

Mum's Engagement Dress, February 2023
From the series *Her Possessions*
Chromogenic print

When she was 15, British photographer Cara Price lost her mother to breast cancer. Having kept many of her belongings, Price began to use these possessions in a series of self-portraits, and is shown here wearing her mother's engagement dress. Creating the portraits allowed Price to connect with her mother while exploring feelings of absence and longing, revisiting memories and seeking closure. She hopes this cathartic process invites others to reflect on their own experiences of loss, grief and remembrance.

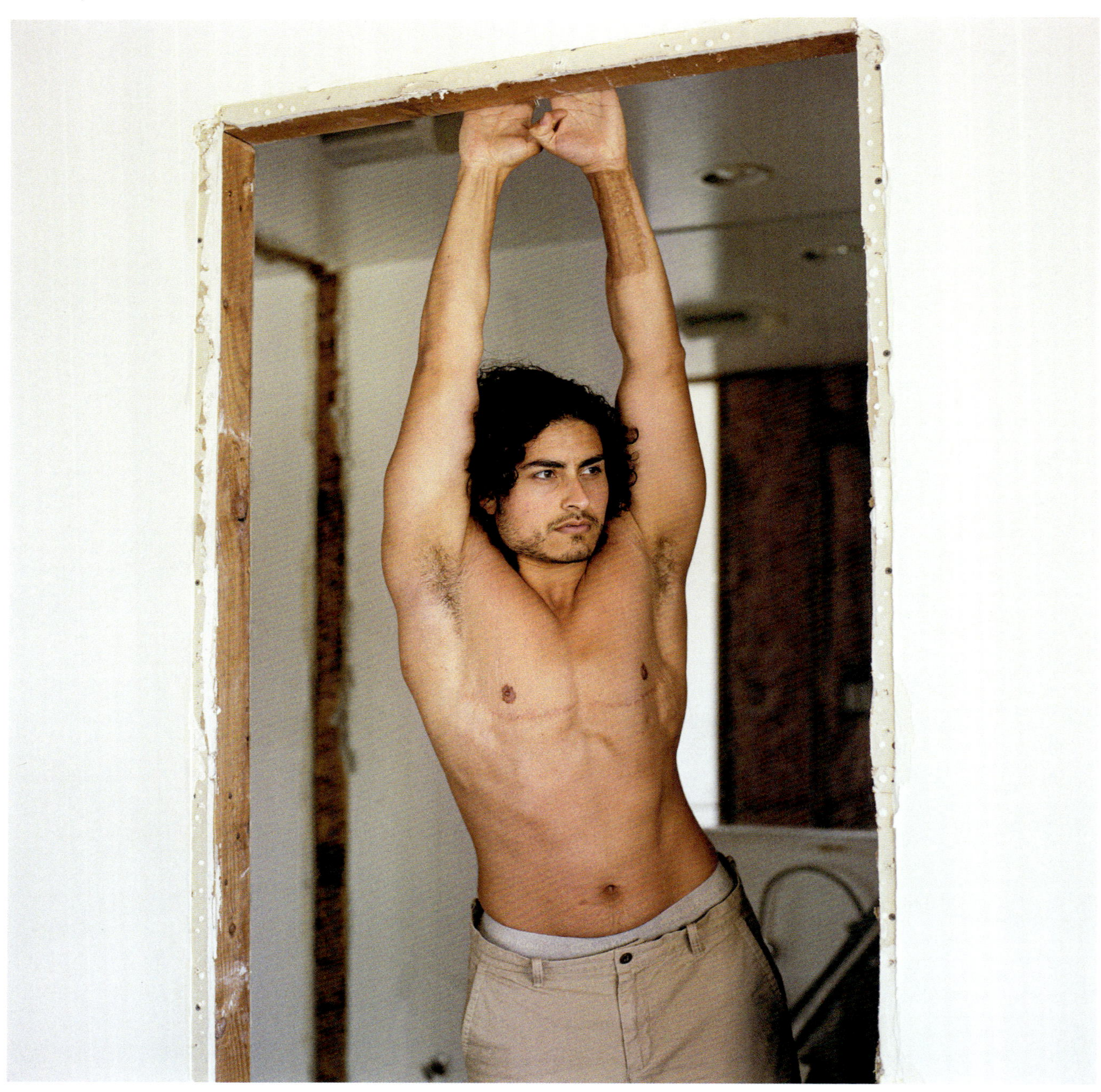

Daniel Zox
Emmett, May 2023
From the series *Always been here,
always will be.*
Chromogenic print

Daniel Zox's portrait of Emmett is part of a series portraying trans sitters. The American artist works collaboratively with the subjects of his portraits to create depictions that challenge popular false narratives. Emmett, who Zox describes as 'kind and proud,' had recently undergone surgery and felt positively about revealing his body. He poses assuredly in front of the camera, while the scars on his chest and wrist communicate a complex journey.

Sophie Wedgwood
Boy on Grass, August 2022
From the series *In Arcadia*
Inkjet print

The result of a fleeting encounter, *Boy on Grass* forms part of a series inspired by the concept of the pastoral paradise of Arcadia, made under 'silvery grey skies and transient light' in parks around the UK by British photographer Sophie Wedgwood. Her series is about escapism and making visible 'imagined worlds under the shadow of uncertain times'. The boy's reclining pose – a trope of art history the photographer knowingly references – is countered by the youthful assurance of his gaze.

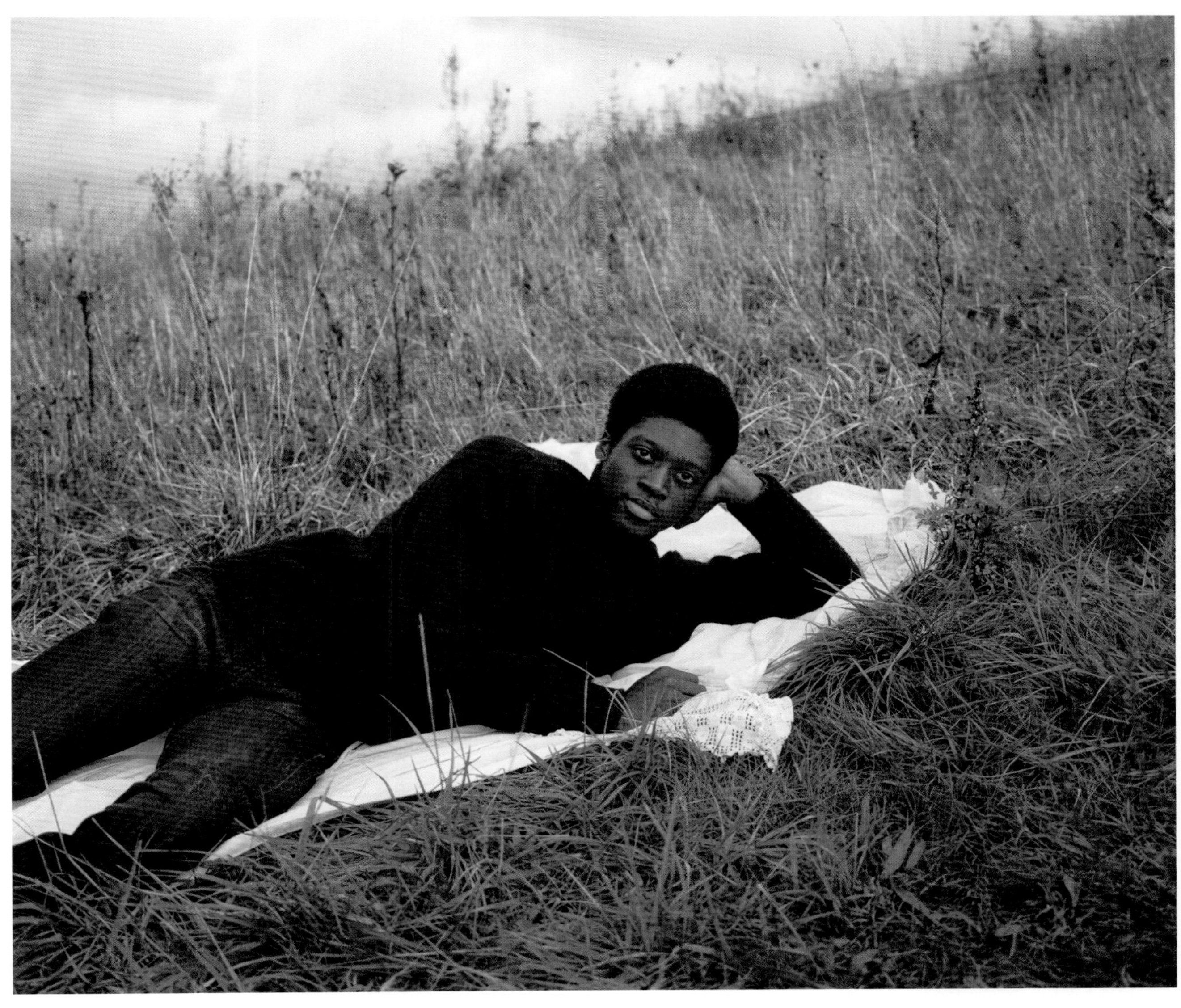

Jenny Lewis
UnBecoming, March 2023
From the series *UnBecoming*
Inkjet print

After photographing her local community for over 20 years, London-based portrait photographer Jenny Lewis turned the camera on herself for the first time. Through an intimate exploration of her experience living with a chronic invisible illness and the unknown territory of menopause, she aims to dissect cultural taboos and open a dialogue about the personal and political aspects of our bodies and lives that often go unseen. 'I realised I felt alien to my own image, coupled with my frustration with the limitations of my body. This work is about finding my way back to myself, transitioning from discomfort to liberation.'

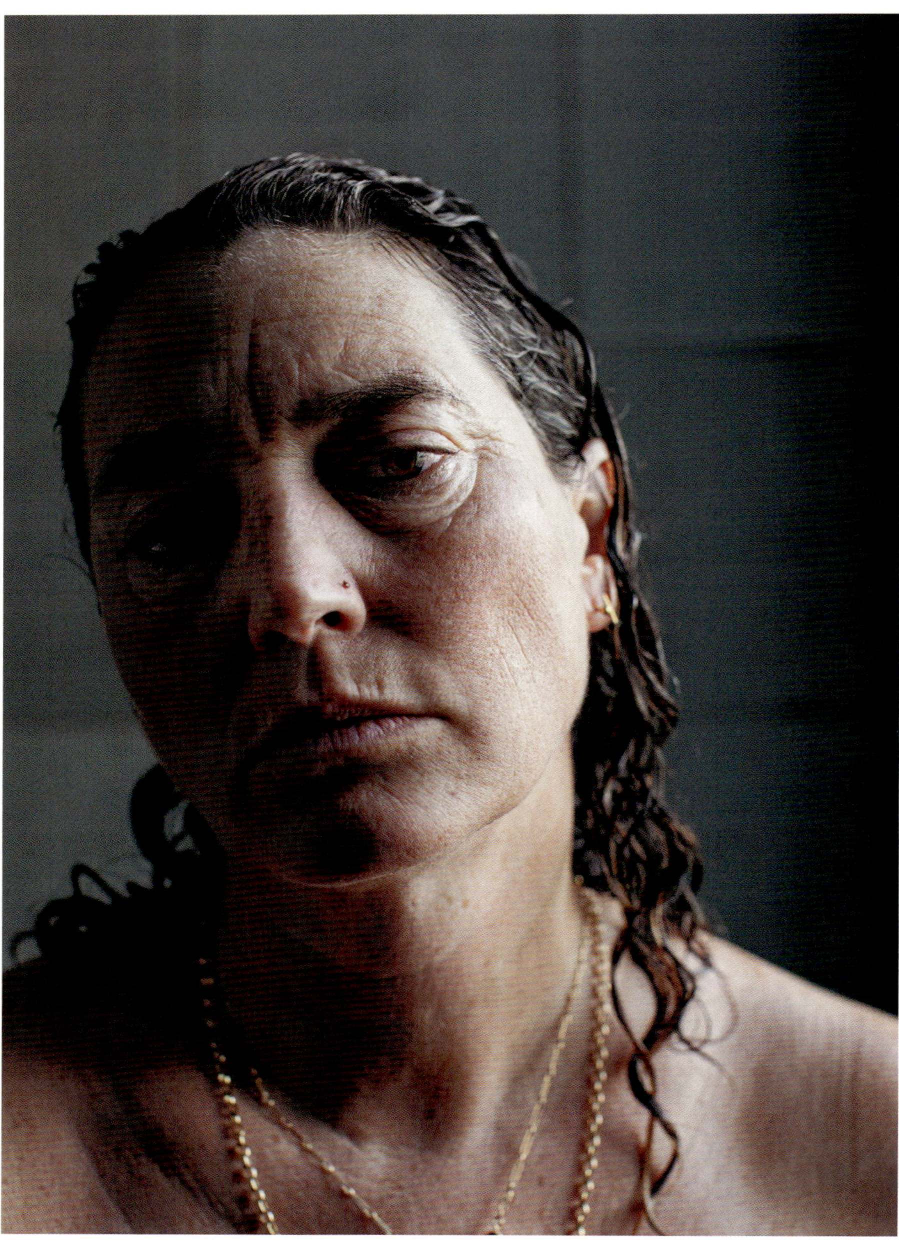

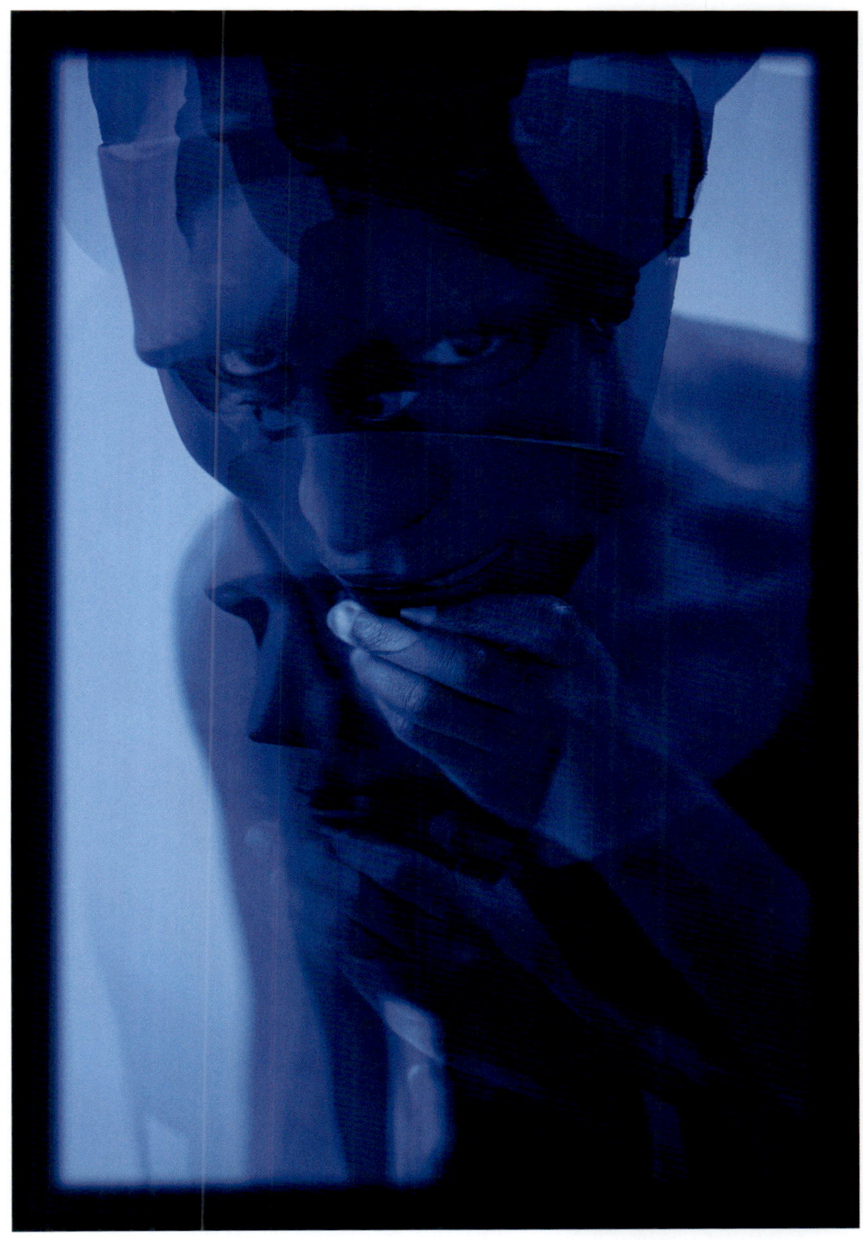

Heather Agyepong
Somebody Stop Me, October 2022
From the series *Ego death*
Chromogenic print

According to psychiatrist Carl Jung, 'the Shadow' comprises aspects of one's personality often shamed and repressed during childhood and adolescence. In this series, British artist and actor Heather Agyepong explores her own shadow, unpacking ideas around shame and observing what she projects onto other people. The blue colour palette of her multi-layered self-portrait is inspired by Tarell Alvin McCraney's play, *In Moonlight Black Boys Look Blue*, symbolising the state of vulnerability needed to transform one's psyche. The series was commissioned by the Jerwood/Photoworks Awards.

D-MO

Fragile Paradise, December 2022
Inkjet print

Polish-Australian photojournalist and visual anthropologist D-MO has been photographing the South Sudanese refugee community in Australia as part of a sustained project to explore how years of displacement have impacted the group's sense of identity. Mother and daughter Akuch and Adhieu have found a place to belong in Australia, building a new life in Sydney and sharing their culture and traditions with the wider community, as memories of their homeland, family and friends become increasingly distant.

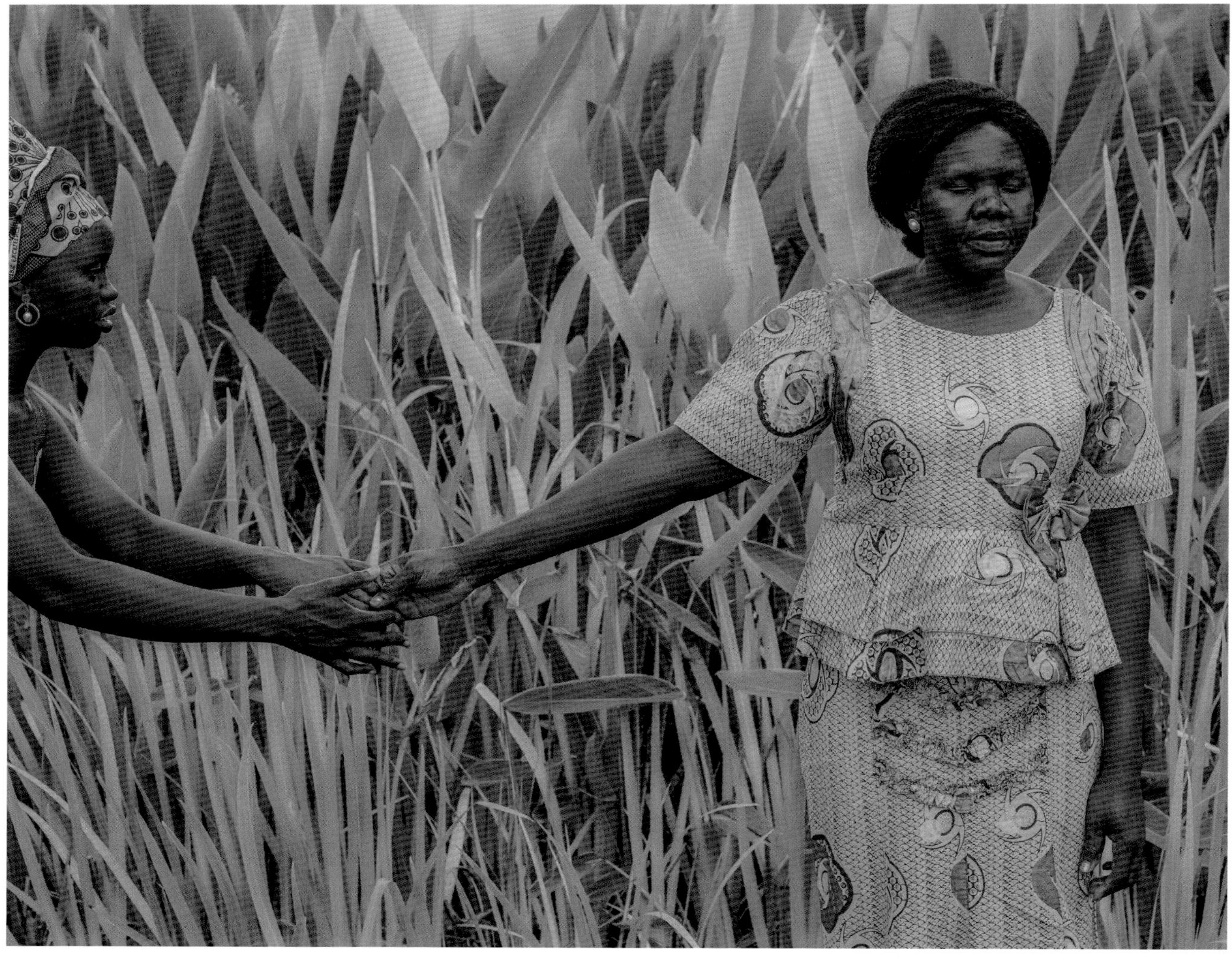

Byron Mohammad Hamzah

Ibu (Mother), December 2022
From the series *Yang Tinggal Hanya Kita
(All That Is Left Is Us)*
Inkjet print

Practicing doctor Byron Mohammad Hamzah grew up in a conservative East-Asian Muslim family in Kuala Lumpur, Malaysia, before moving to the UK to study medicine. His mother, Farah, found it difficult to come to terms with her son's decision. 'As time passed,' Hamzah notes, 'I could see that our values and views of life had changed, and so had the dynamics of our relationship.' His intimate portrait explores the complexities of his relationship with his mother, 'the stoic matriarch' of the family.

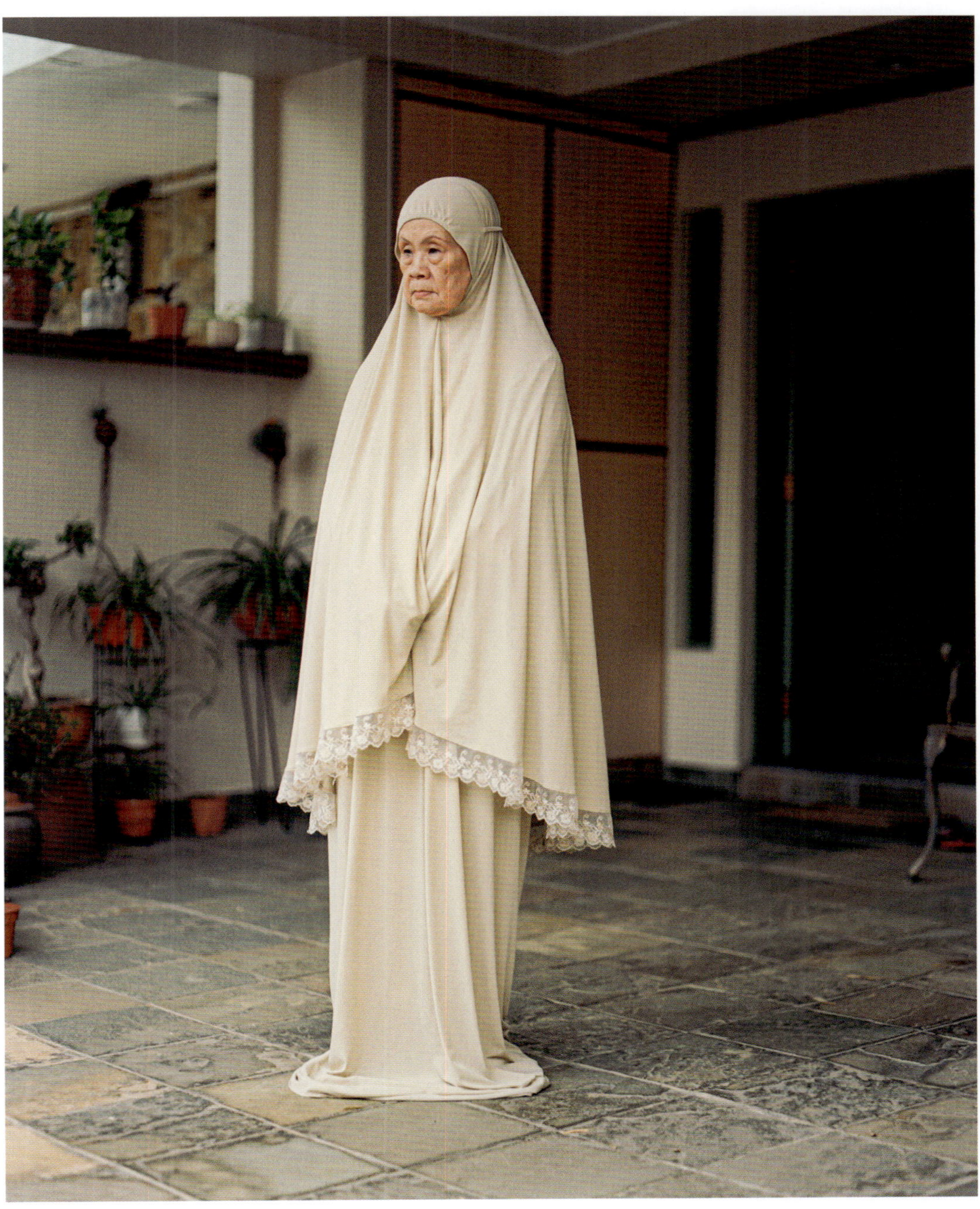

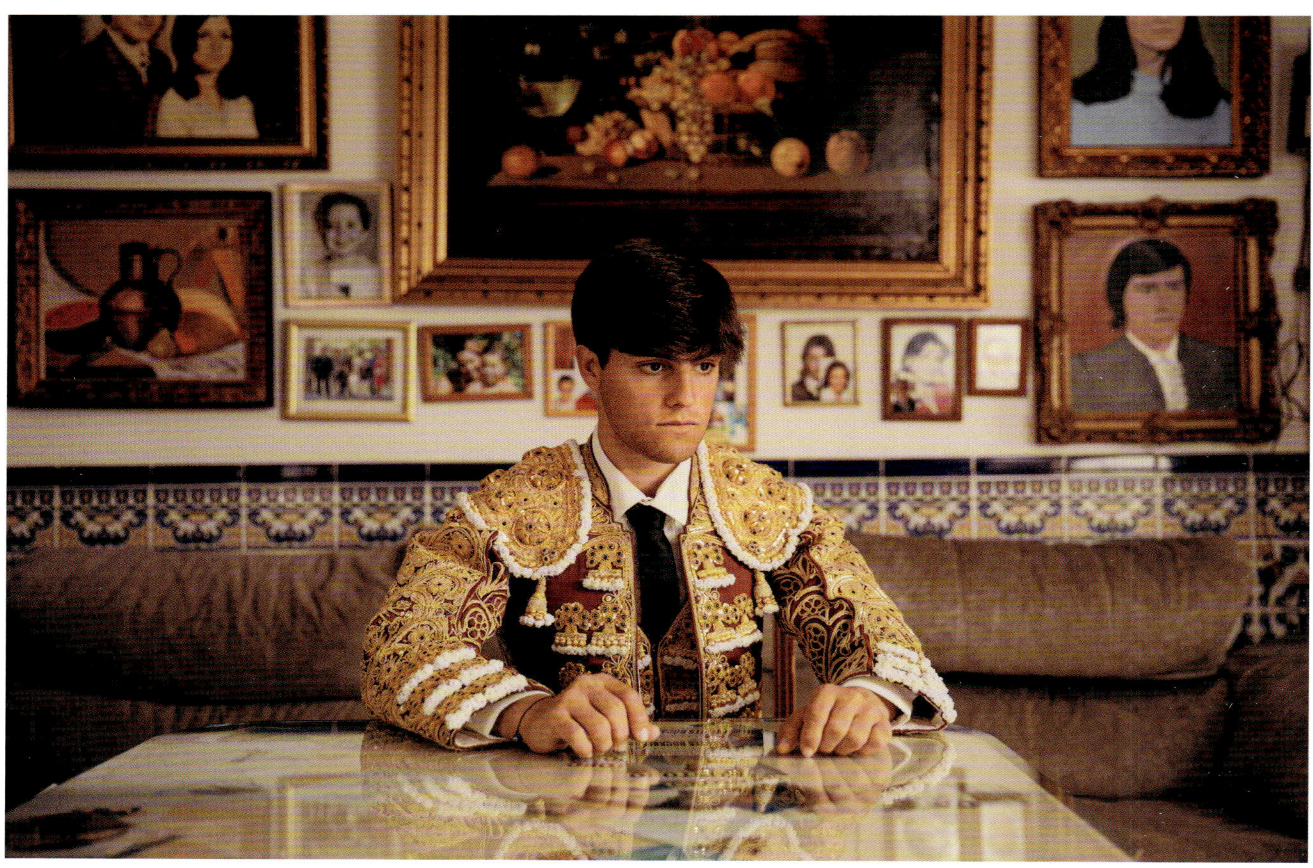

Owen Harvey

David Fuentes, a young trainee Novillero, with ambitions of becoming a popular Matador,
March 2023
From the series *The Matador*
Chromogenic print

This portrait of *novillero* (aspiring bullfighter) David Fuentes is part of a series documenting young matadors in which London-based photographer Owen Harvey explores notions of identity and masculinity alongside Spain's much-debated bullfighting tradition. Photographed in his familial home in Córdoba, Fuentes wears an embroidered *traje de luces* (suit of light) made by his grandfather, a dresser for bullfighters. He is surrounded by portraits of relatives who, together, form a long line of bullfighters. Harvey's portrait invites the viewer to reflect on a rich history facing an uncertain future.

Carl Francois van der Linde

Dev Dangi, February 2023
From the series *Our Leader*
Inkjet print

South African photographer Carl Francois van der Linde photographed Dev Dangi posed on his bed at a wrestling academy in Jalandhar, India. Sleeping eight to a room, the wrestlers' privacy in the barrack-style accommodation is limited, but comradery remains high. Environmental details provide clues to the aspirations of the sitter: a poster of American WWE wrestler John Cena can be seen crudely taped to the wall, above a string of laundry, together with a duvet cover featuring the word 'dreams.'

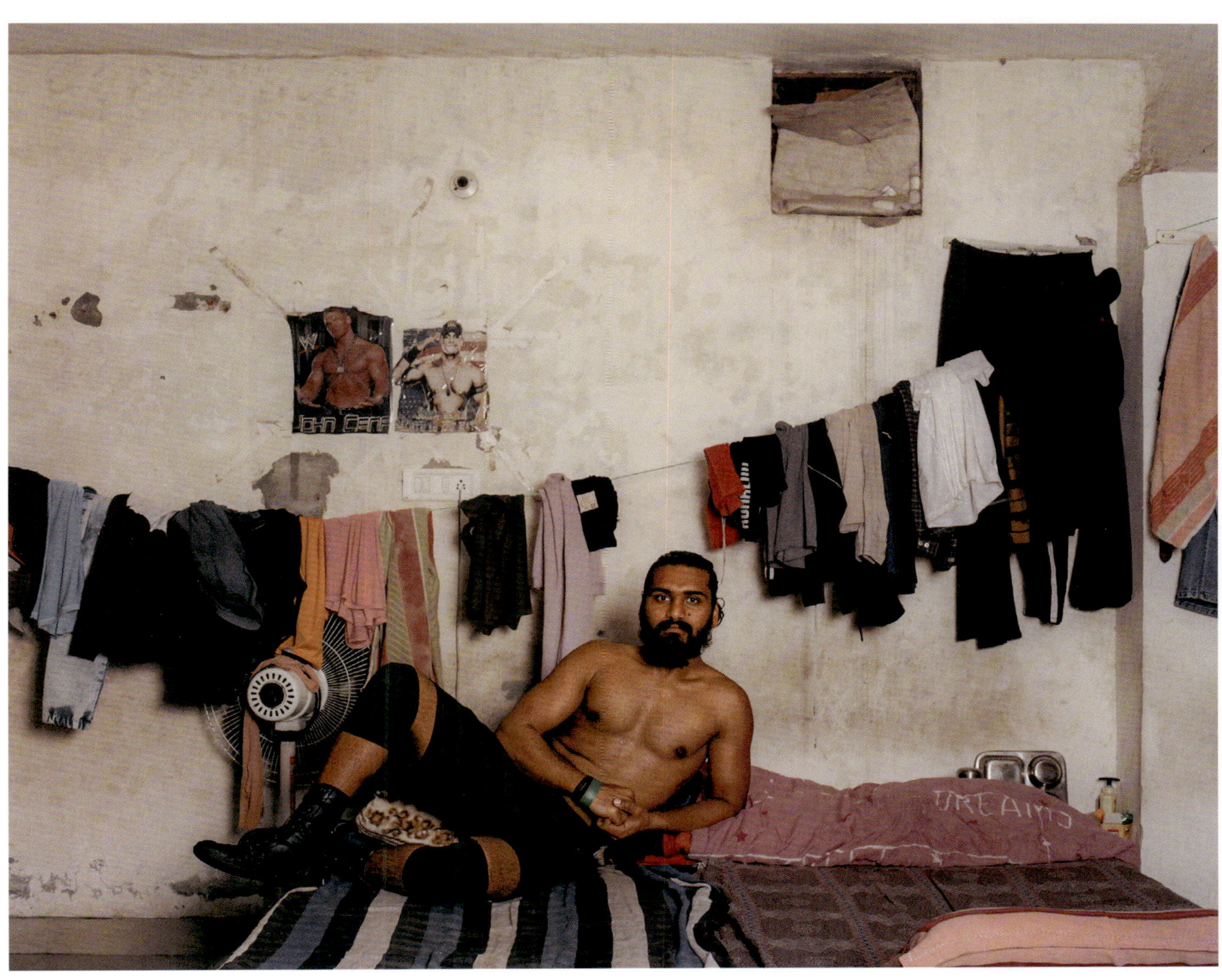

Sridhar Balasubramaniyam

Untitled, May 2022
Untitled, June 2022
From the series *Space Between Us*
Chromogenic prints

Having worked with the post-modern theatre group Manal Magudi, Indian photographer Sridhar Balasubramaniyam developed 'an awareness of the body as a medium' and began a project to photograph the performances of theatre artists in the landscapes of southern India. Balasubramaniyam's long-term collaborators Charles and Eswaran are posed in the city of Madurai. With their faces obscured, the photographs explore the form and movement of the men's bodies in union with the spirit and history of the landscape.

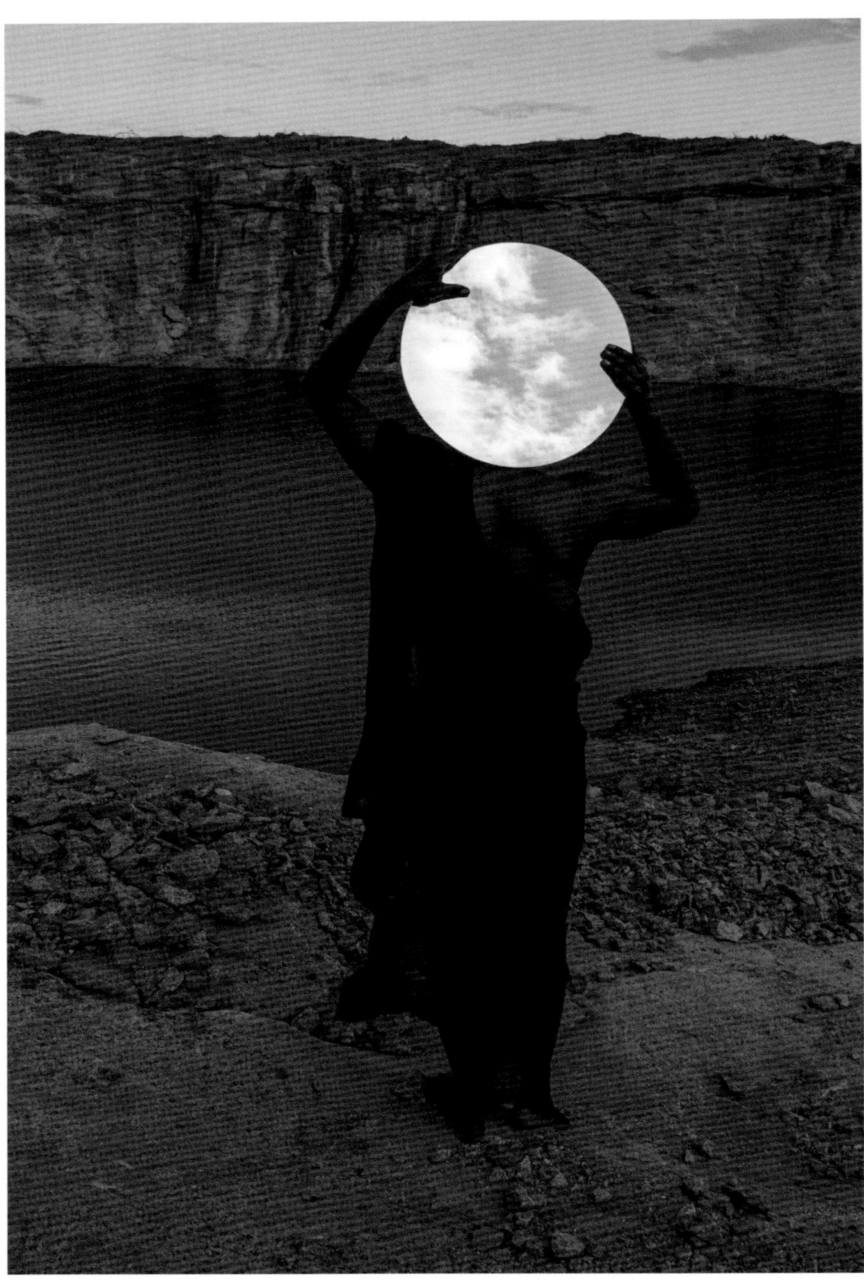

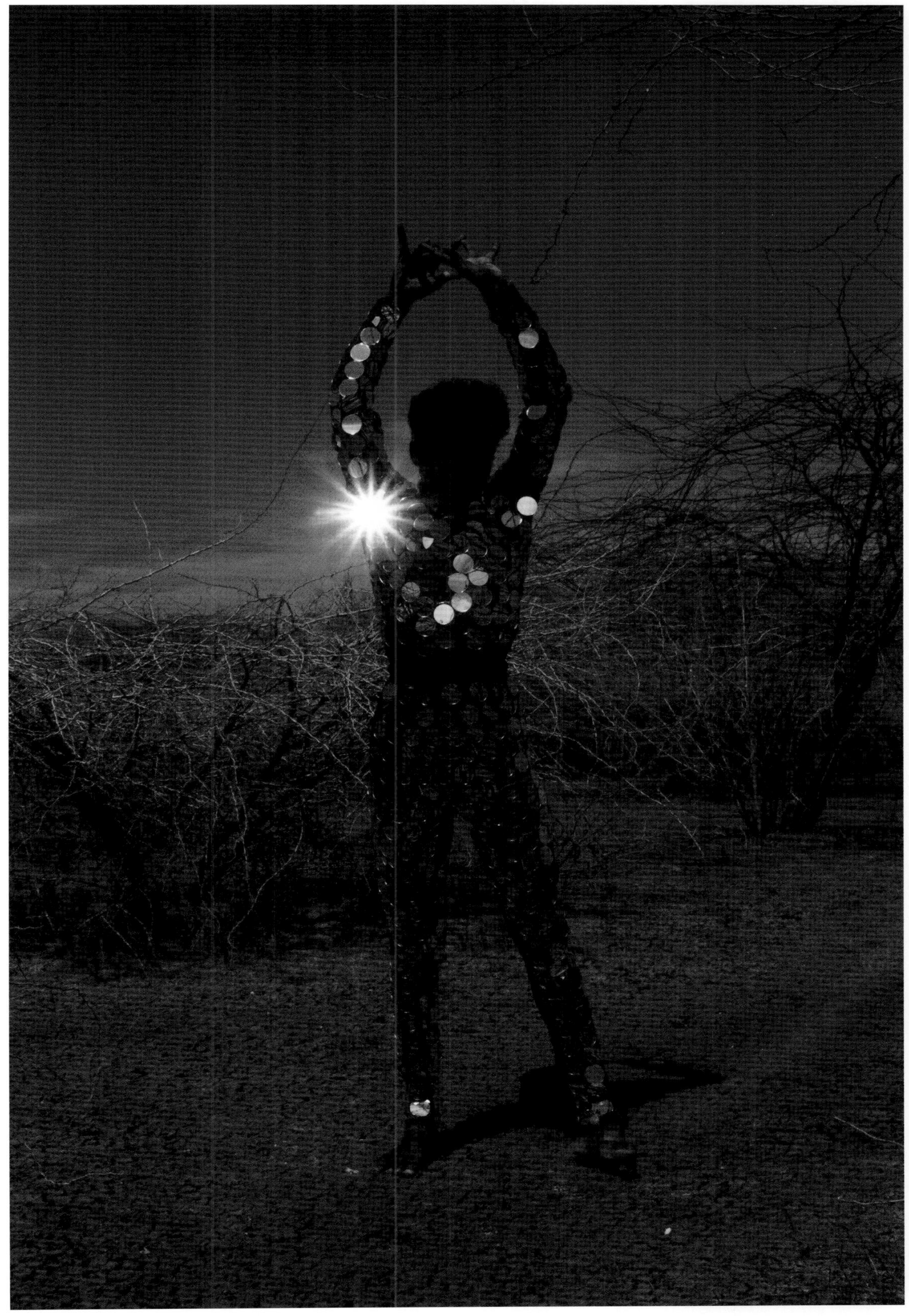

Ed Alcock

Jessica swatting flies, Tricastin,
September 2022
From the series *Risk Zones*
Chromogenic print

Jessica grew up within a few hundred meters of the Tricastin nuclear power station in south-east France. Franco-British Ed Alcock was commissioned by the Bibliothèque Nationale de France (French National Library) to document the inhabitants of risk zones – areas within five kilometres of a nuclear plant. Amid the revival of nuclear energy, and against the backdrop of the war in Ukraine, where nuclear installations have become military targets, Alcock wanted to understand whether inhabitants are aware of the dangers they face.

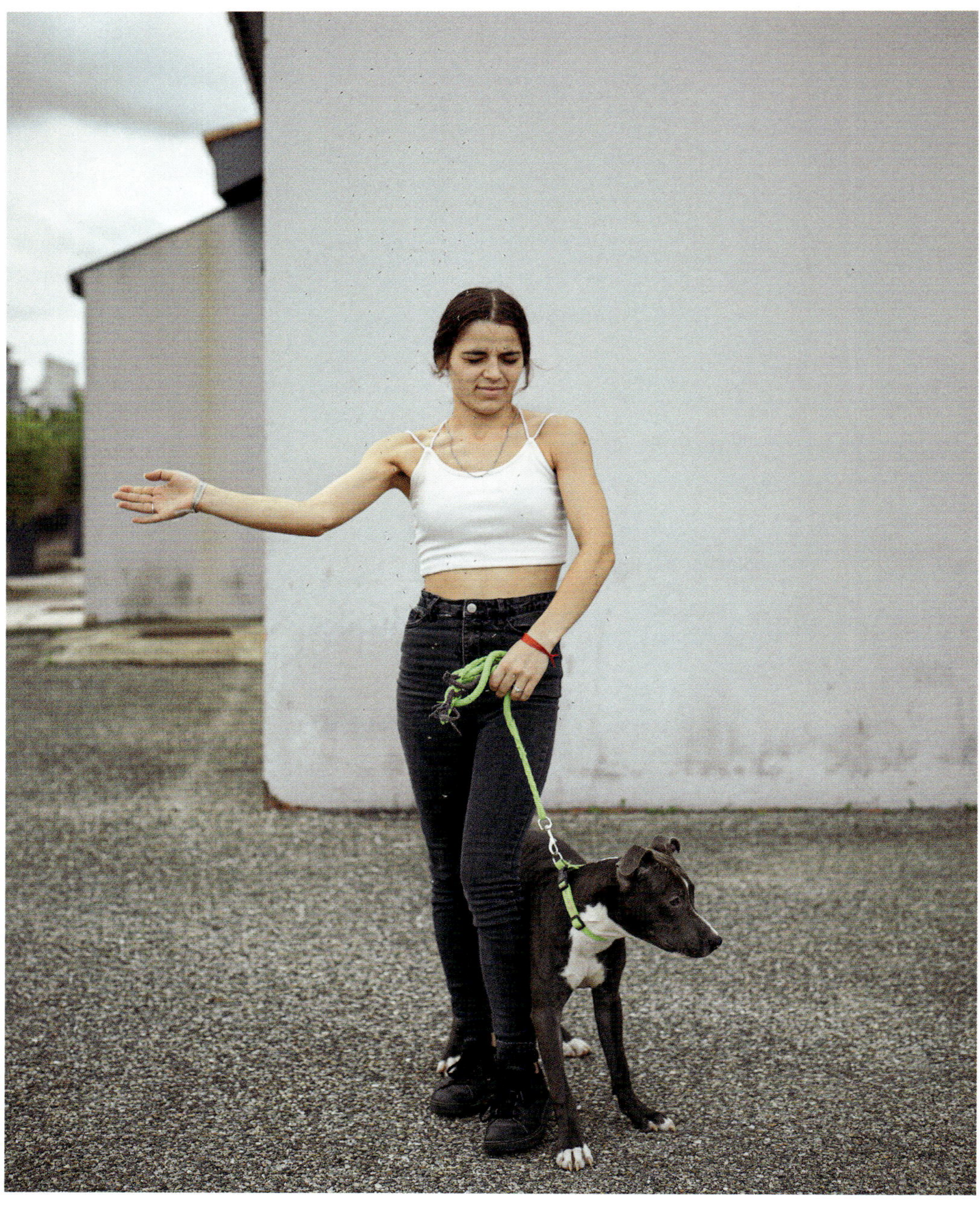

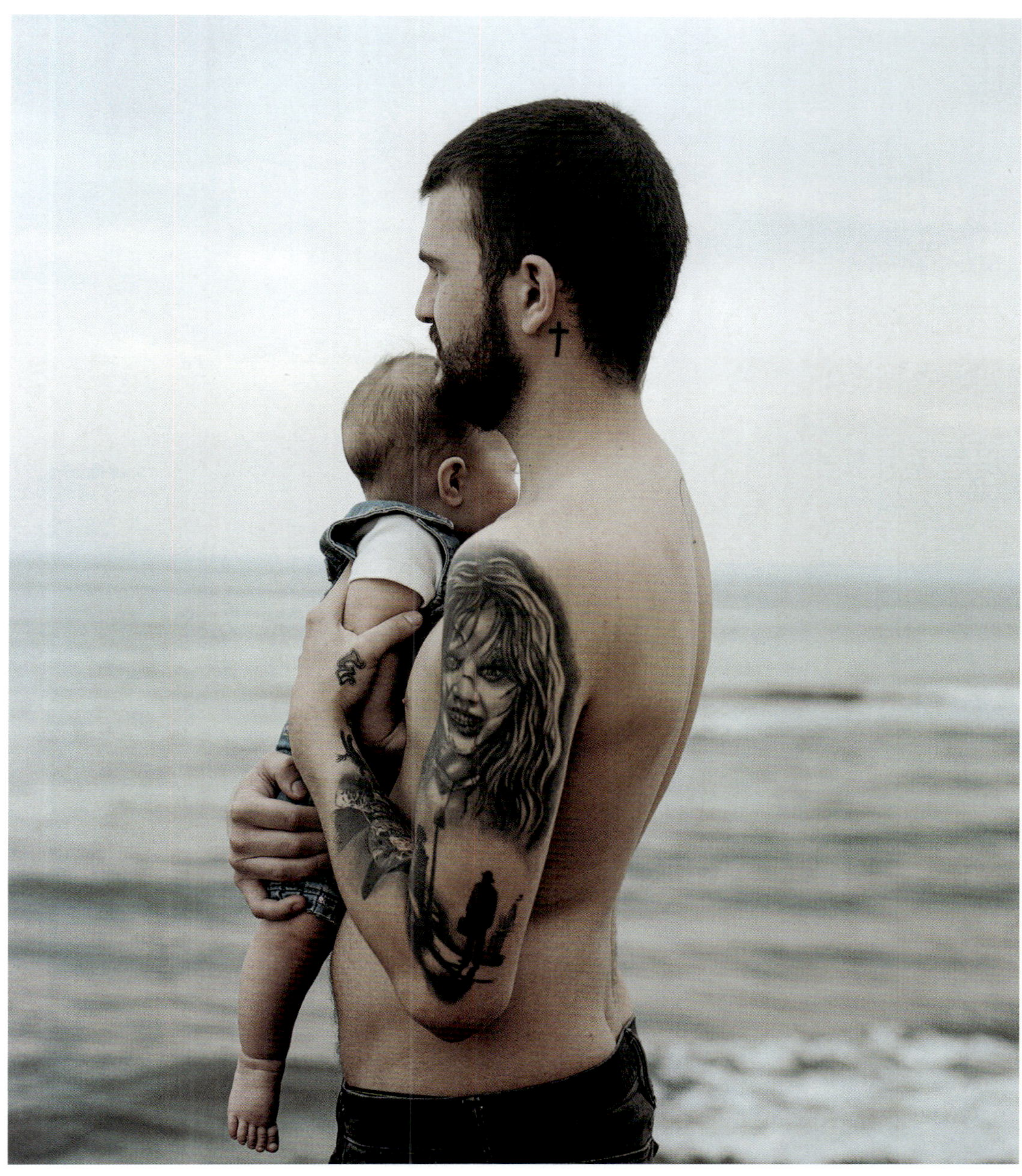

Harry Compton

Tanner and Baby Eleanor, August 2022
From the series *The Sunny Side of the Island*
Inkjet print

In the series *The Sunny Side of the Island*, British photographer Harry Compton uses portraits and historical records to explore the legacy of his ancestor and namesake, Colonel Harry Compton, who was gifted a township in Prince Edward Island, Canada, by King George III as compensation for his participation in the Irish Rebellion of 1798. This portrait shows two residents of Prince Edward Island, Tanner and his daughter Eleanor, who are related to both Colonel Compton and the photographer on parallel lines of descent. 'We were both complete strangers but family all the same,' Compton explains.

Thomas Duffield

Grandad Sups his Tea, March 2022
Inkjet print

During weekly home visits in Leeds, British photographer and researcher Thomas Duffield has been making portraits of his maternal grandfather, Fred, as he approaches his ninetieth birthday. In the absence of a father figure, Duffield's grandfather played a primary caregiving role in his life and has become a recurring presence in his photographic practice. Looking for beauty in the everyday, Duffield caught Fred as he lifted a steaming cup of milky tea to his mouth.

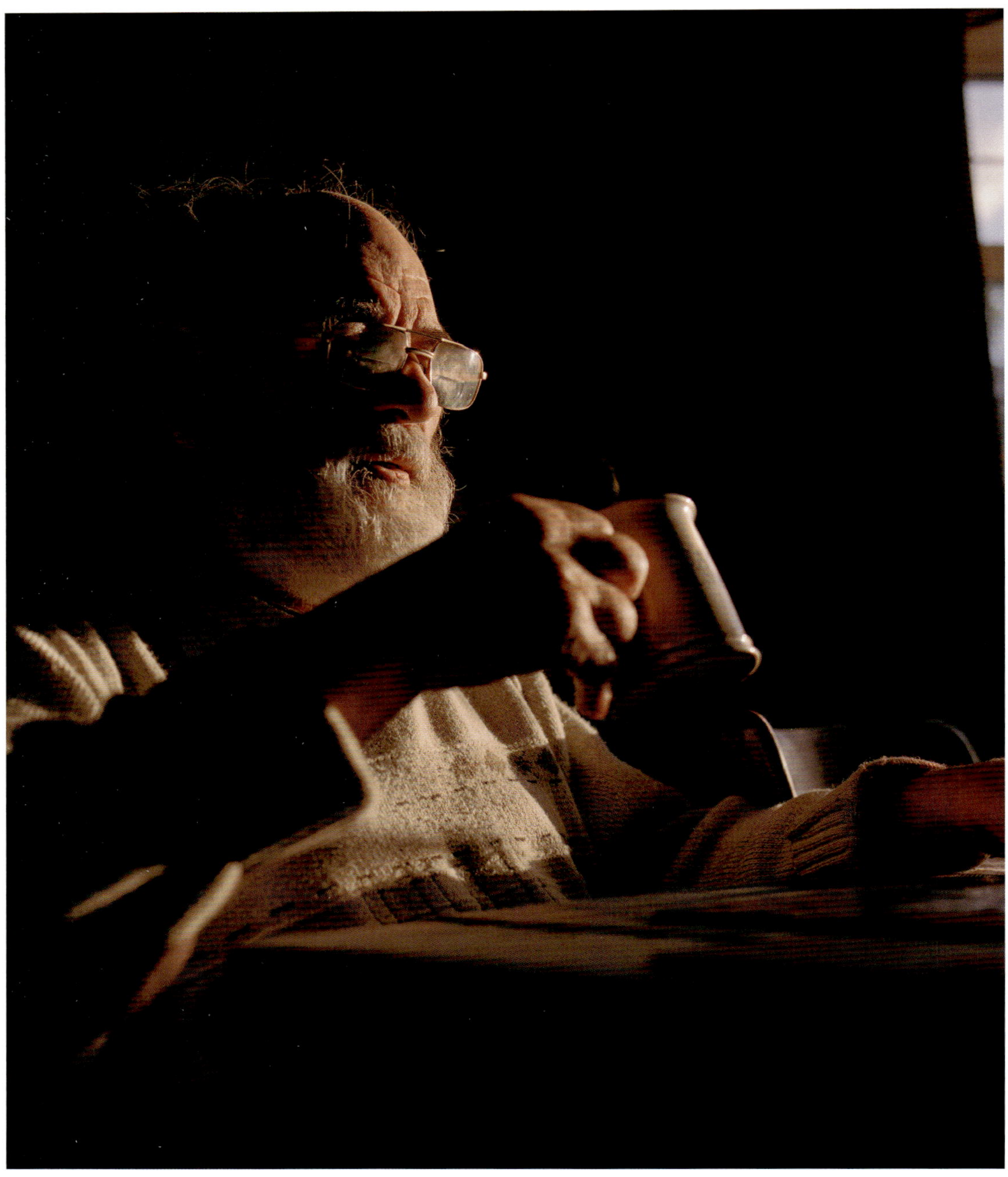

Benjamin Madgwick

Bartholomé and Pandora #13, December 2022
From the series *Relationships*
Chromogenic print

The series *Relationships* is a collaboration between British photographer Benjamin Madgwick and casting director Emma Somper to 'explore the diverse tapestry of human connections and the profound significance they hold in our lives.' Bartholomé, a British model and actor, was photographed for the series alongside his sister Pandora, also a model. Pictured here by himself, against a minimalist background and bathed in soft light, the lack of extraneous detail allows the sitter's authenticity to shine.

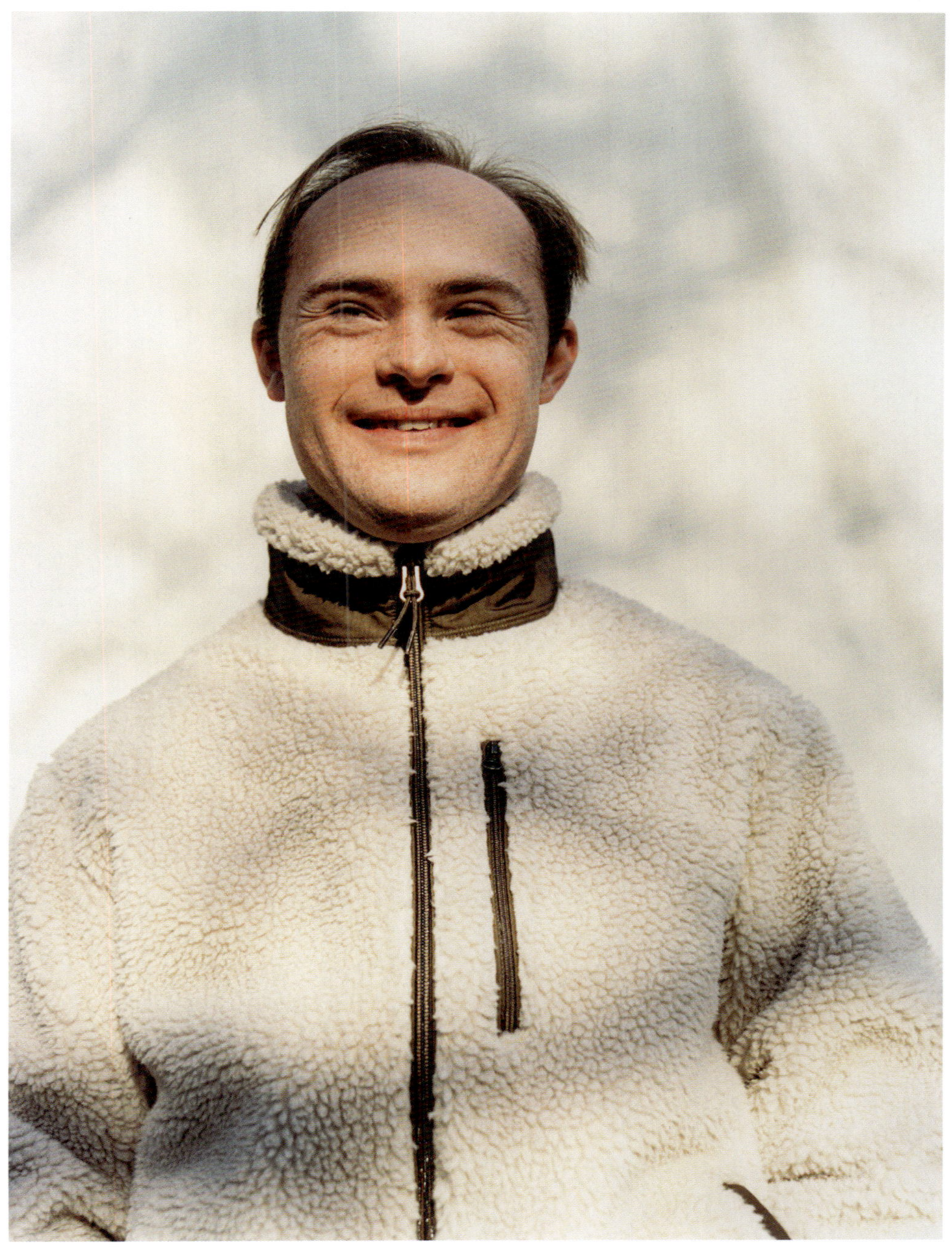

Ana Paganini
Our Lady of Fatima waiting to be directed,
August 2022
Our Lady of Hope, August 2022
From the series *Jesus' Blood Never Failed Me Yet*
Inkjet prints

Portuguese photographer Ana Paganini has been documenting the spectacle of religious processions as part of a long-term project to explore the influence of Catholic rituals and traditions on the lives of Portuguese teenagers. The square frame of her medium format camera enables Paganini to focus on specific individuals within the crowds. Here, young girls dressed in rented costumes impersonate Catholic saints, with poses reminiscent of religious sculptures. Their performances are undercut by small details, such as vividly painted nails, which bring a contemporary moment to an otherwise traditional scene.

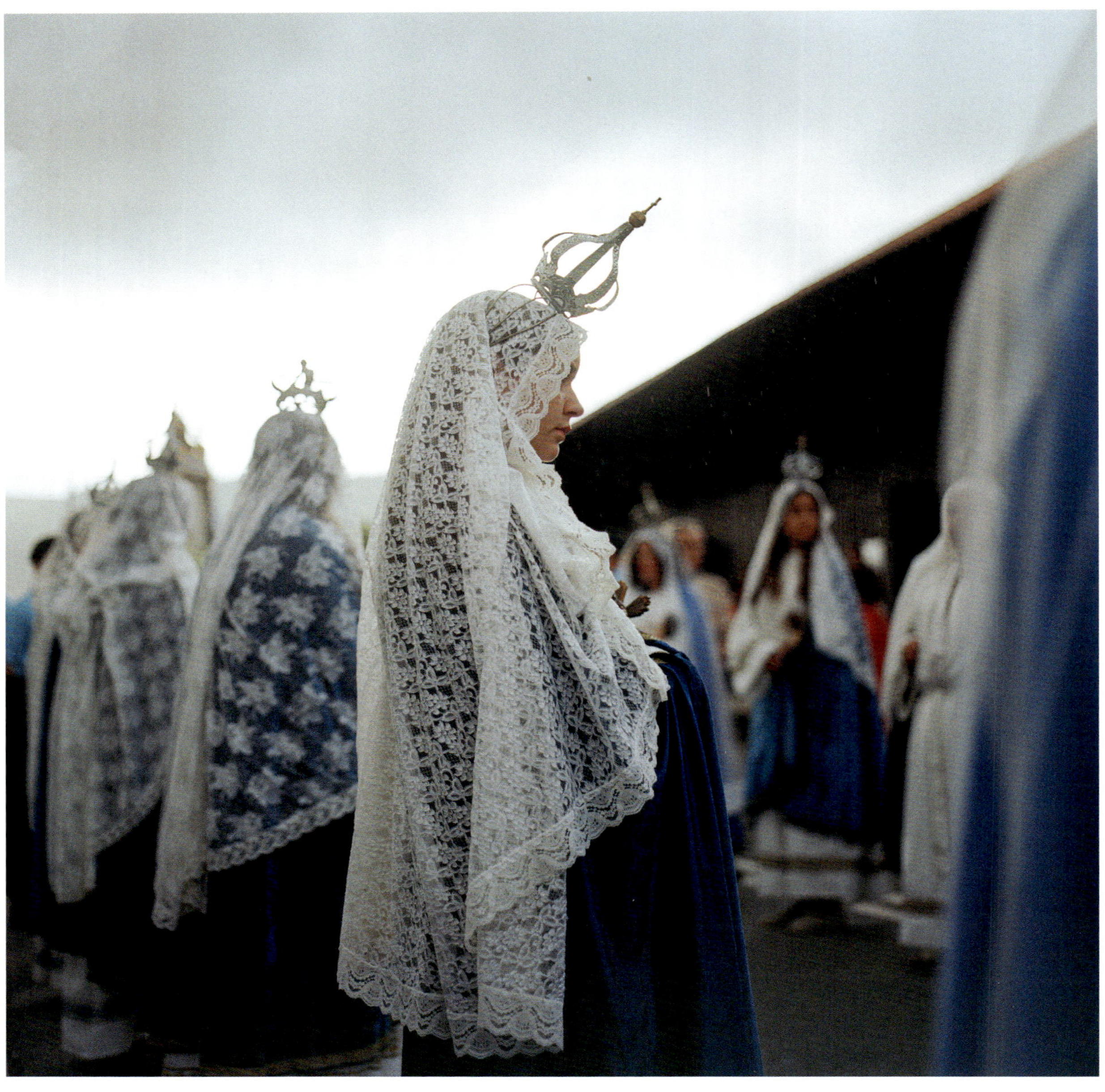

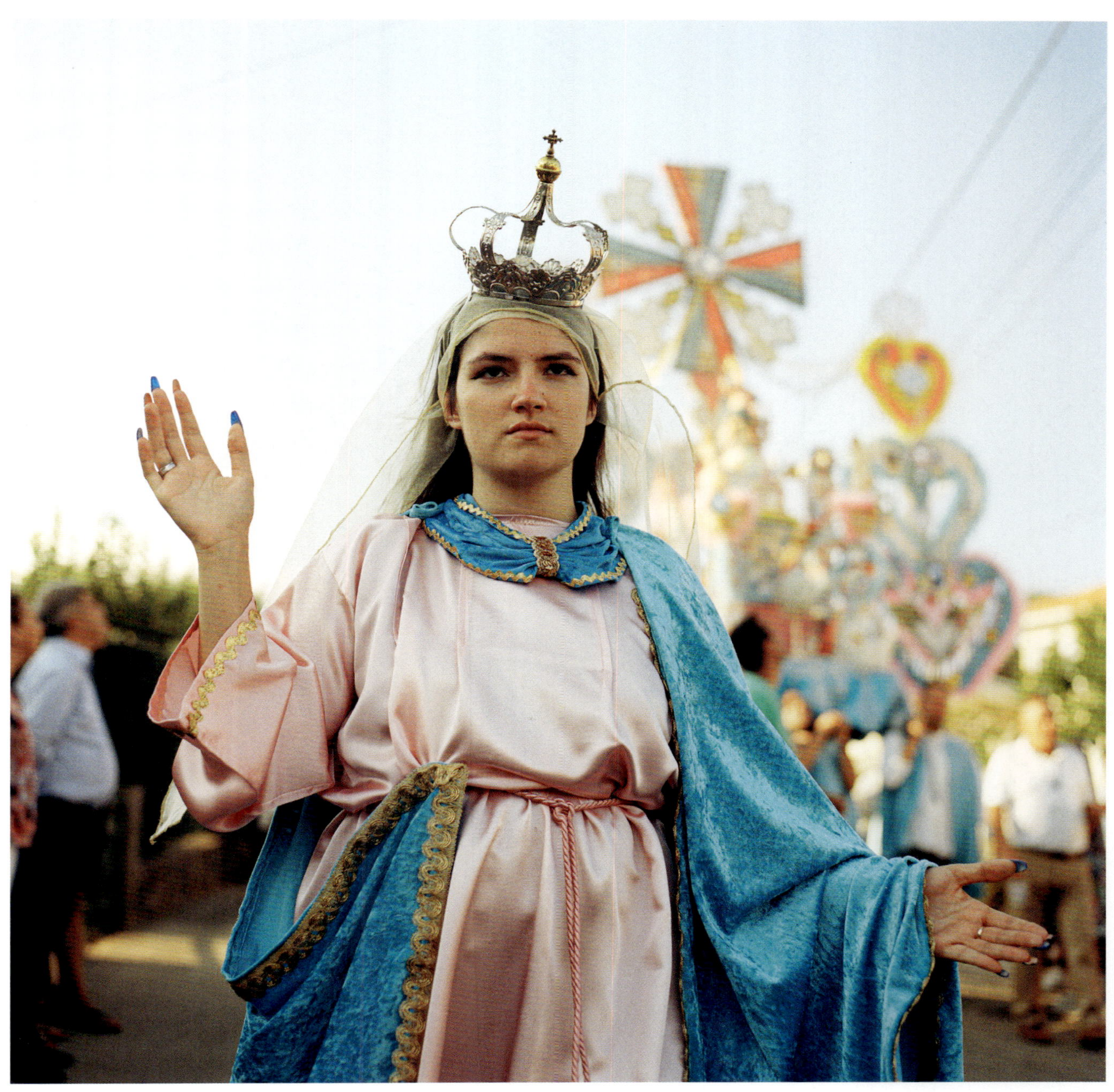

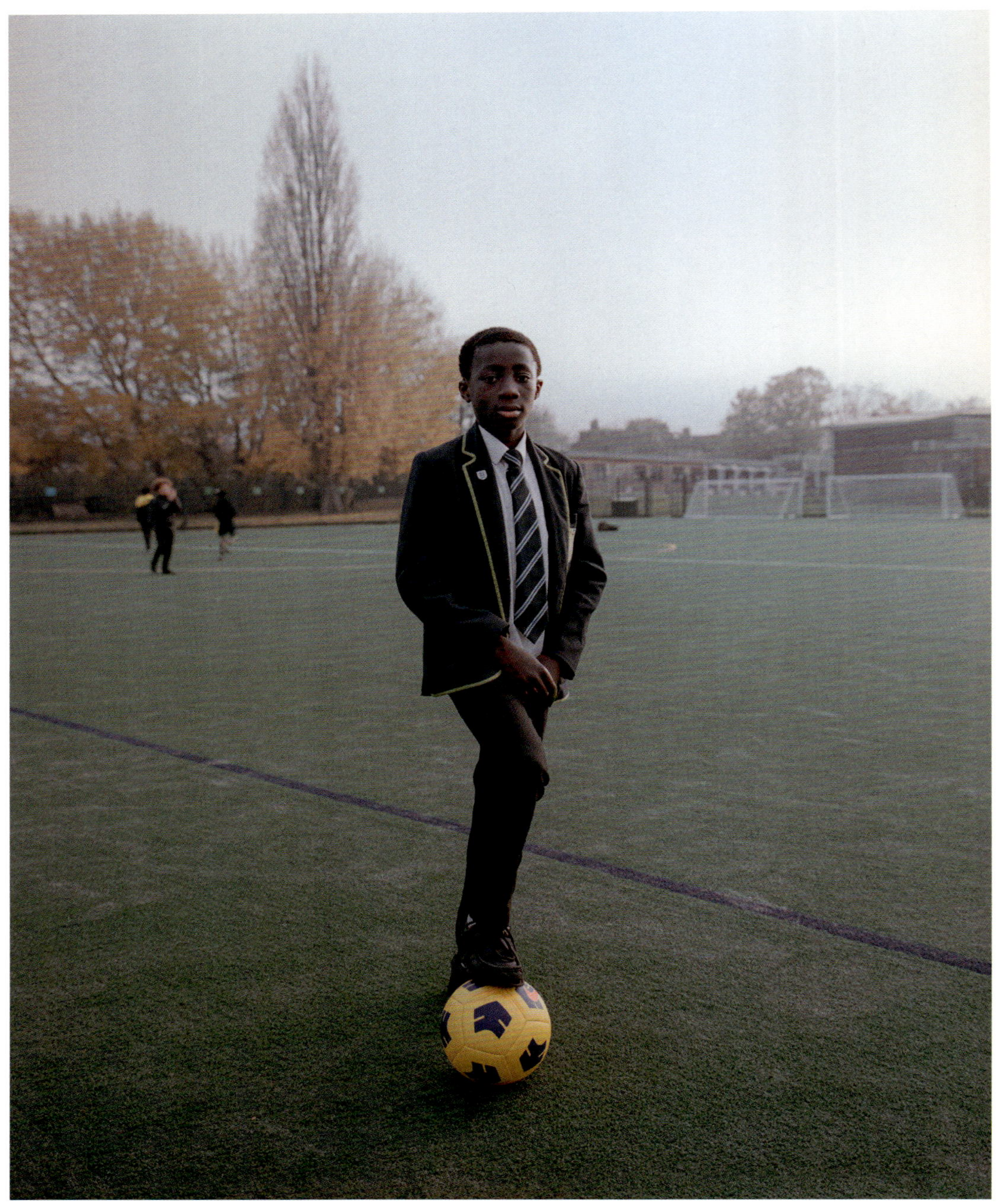

Ben Brooks

Three Lions, December 2022
From the series *Losing the Dressing Room*
Chromogenic print

British photographer Ben Brooks has been photographing secondary school students in London who are participating in Football Beyond Borders, a programme that supports young people to positively shape their futures by building on their passion for football. Brooks wanted to capture the range of personalities within the football teams and took a number of individual portraits, including this image of Shadrach. He explains, 'it reinstated the importance of giving young people space to express themselves.'

Francesca Mills

A moment's pause, July 2022
From the series *Good Evening We Are From Ukraine*
Chromogenic print

Devon-based photographer Francesca Mills has been photographing Ukrainian families uprooted by the Russian invasion as part of a project that examines 'our collective need for home and community.' Mills first met 9-year-old Artem and his family in the summer of 2022, when they arrived in Devon under the UK's Homes for Ukraine scheme. Looking unusually apprehensive as he stood on the threshold of the swimming pool, Mills noted, 'Artem's hesitation made me think of every other moment his family had stopped to make impossible decisions during their journey from Ukraine.'

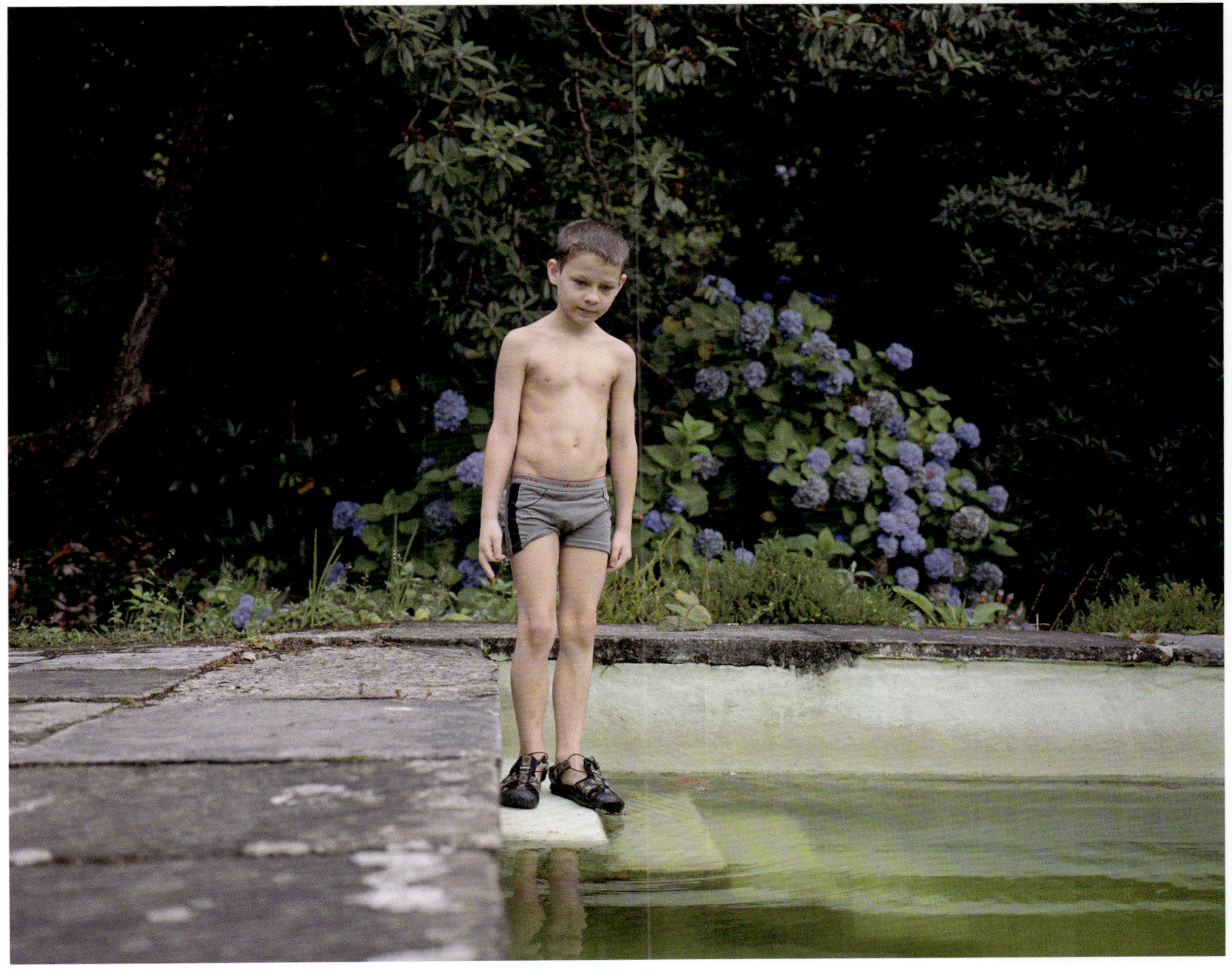

Alice Zoo

Joanna Bell, NHS nurse, on the hottest day ever recorded, July 2022
Chromogenic print

London-based photographer and writer Alice Zoo was working on assignment for the *New York Times* when she made this portrait of NHS nurse Joanna Bell. The story was about essential work through the record-breaking heatwave that hit London in summer 2022. Joanna relayed to Zoo how the air conditioning had broken down in the A&E ward – the extreme heat adding to the exhaustion of the medical staff.

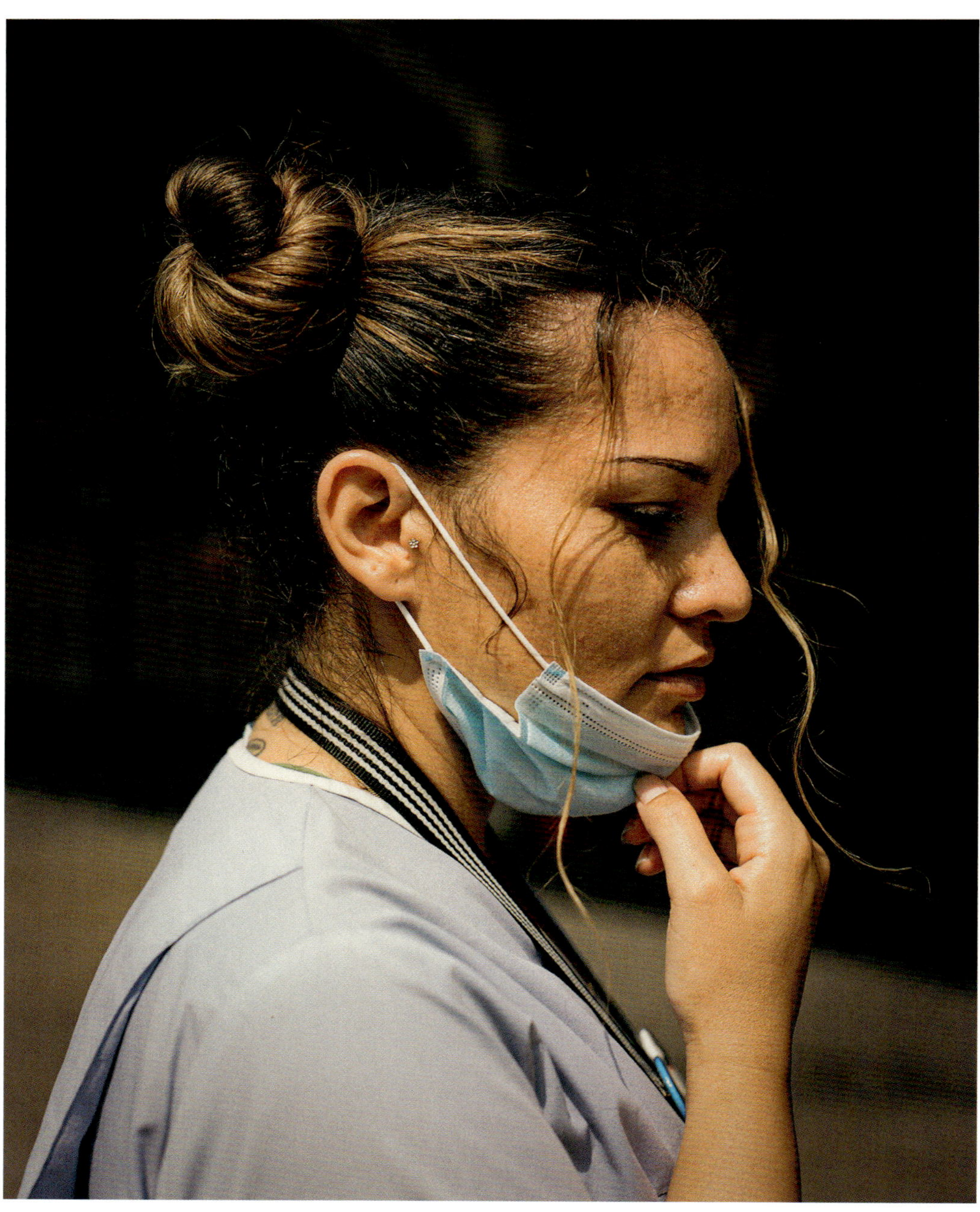

Mustafah Abdulaziz

Jose, former Angolan child soldier.
Cape Town, South Africa, March 2023
From the series *Identität*
Chromogenic print

Jose is photographed remembering and recounting his experience of abduction at the age of 15, when he was forced to become a child soldier in Angola. He dreamt of running away and escaped one night, travelling thousands of kilometres on foot to South Africa. Now living in Cape Town, he runs every day up a mountain overlooking the sea. Berlin-based photographer Mustafa Abdulaziz aims to capture something of the inner world of his sitters in his compassionate portraiture. Jose recounted, 'In life, don't be afraid. Just be free.'

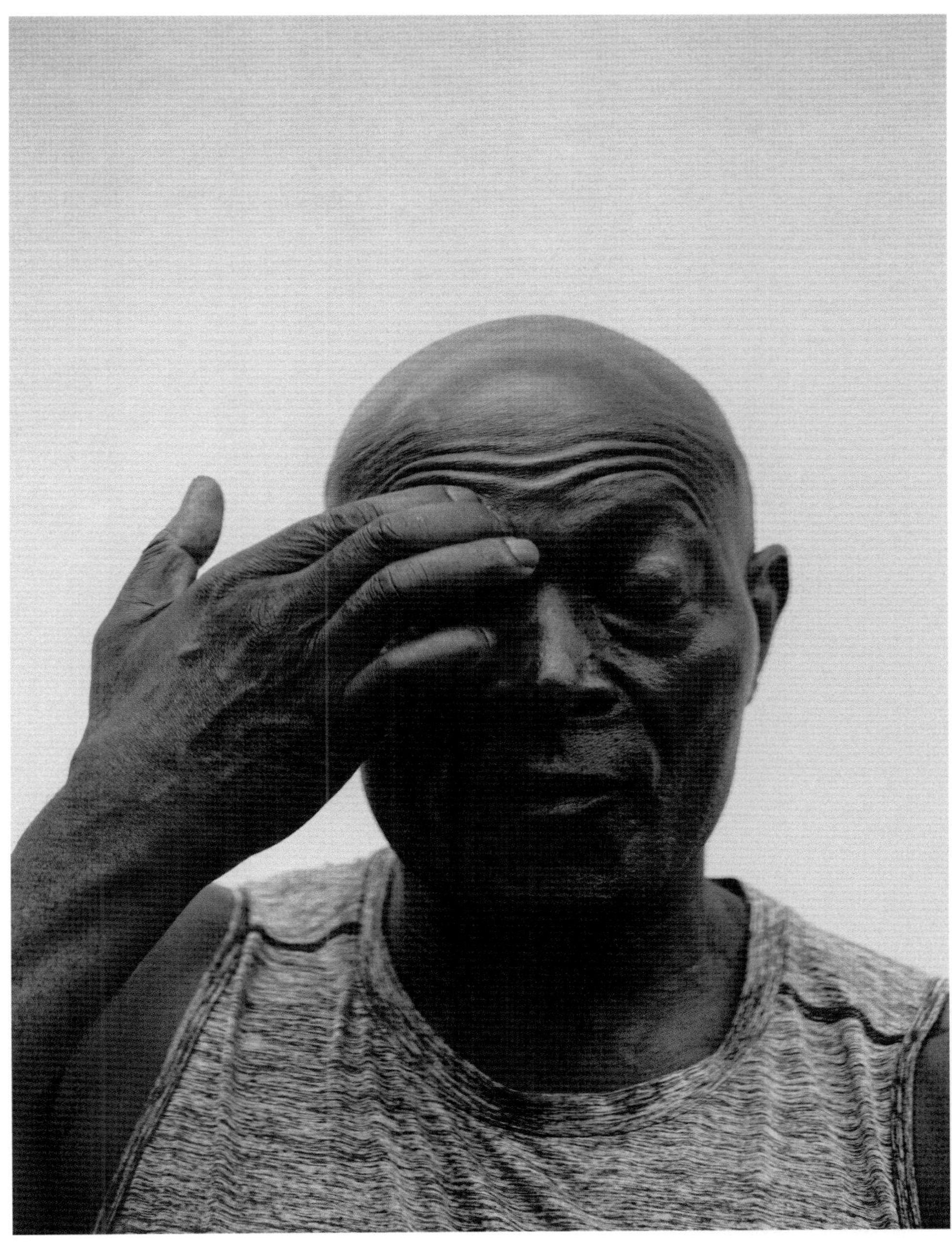

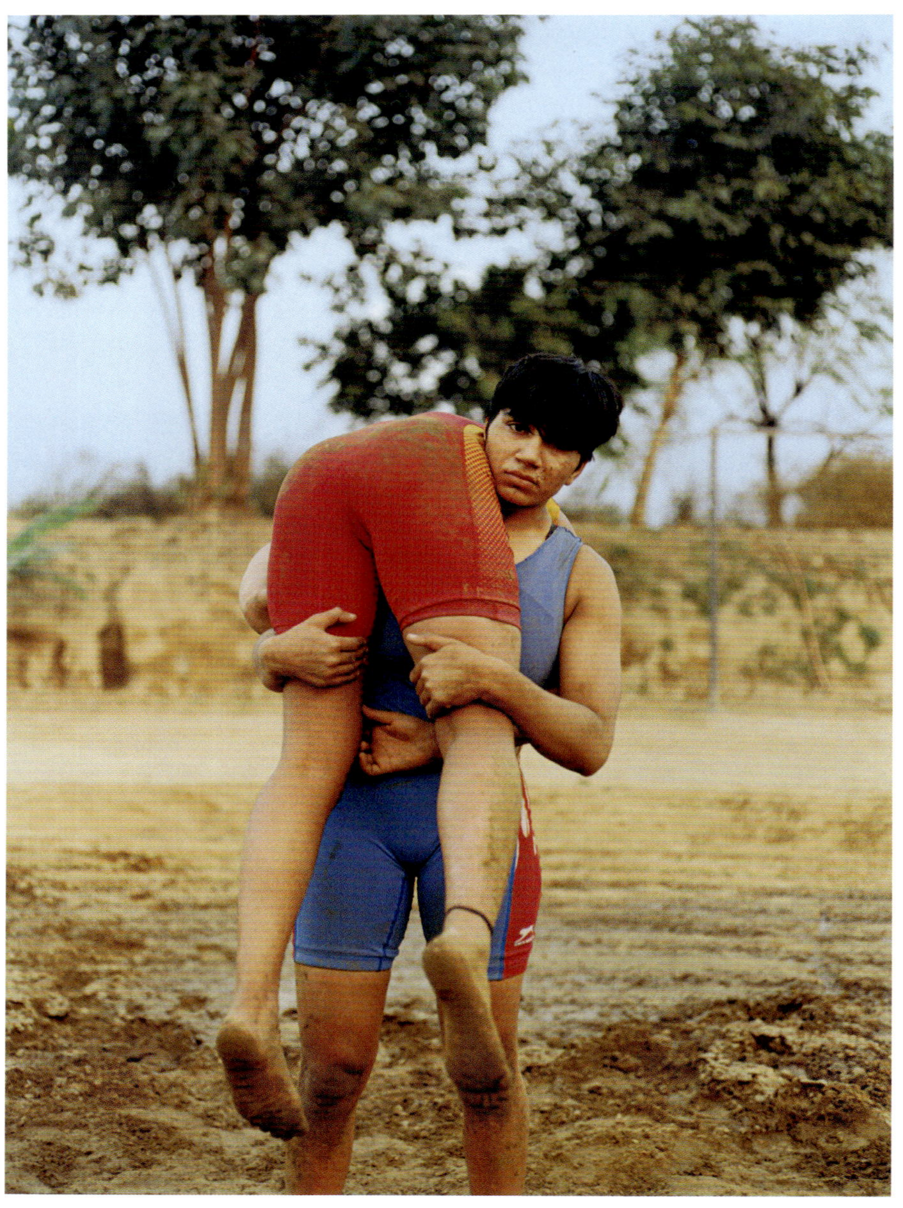

Prarthna Singh
The Wrestlers, November 2022
From the series *Champion*
Chromogenic print

Bombay-based photographer Prarthna Singh photographed sports training camps, where young women train to be wrestlers, in the north-central Indian states of Haryana and Uttar Pradesh. These states are also known for high rates of crimes against women, female infanticide and child marriage. Within the camps, girls occupy traditionally male-dominated spaces, determined to change their destinies as they evolve into competent wrestlers and strong, empathetic women. Their powerful bodies offer a counterpoint to institutionalised patriarchy, which leaves little space for representation outside prescribed ideas of femininity.

Roberto Alegria

Bodybuilder, May 2022
Chromogenic print

Born in Ghana, Patrick Asiedu migrated to Italy before settling in Sydney. Having overcome addiction to achieve success as a professional bodybuilder, Asiedu is determined to realise his ambition of winning the prestigious title Mr. Olympia. His sculpted physique stands in contrast to the subtle backdrop of soft clouds in Spanish photographer Roberto Alegria's studio portrait, which sought to 'convey the incredible strength and unwavering determination of a man who faced a challenging past but now envisions a future filled with hope and promise.'

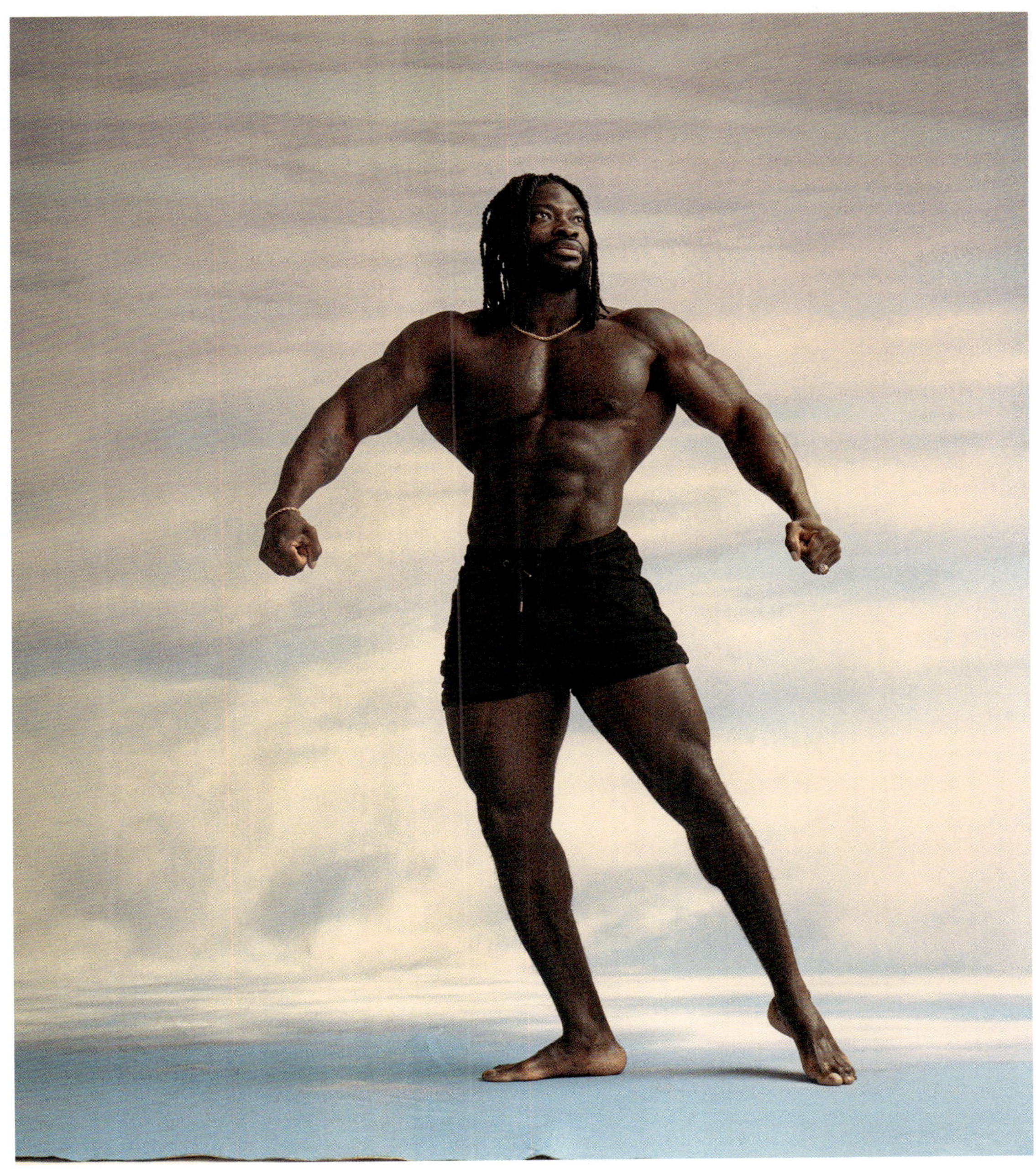

In Focus Photographer Hassan Hajjaj

Since 2015, the In Focus display has showcased new work by acclaimed photographers, including Alessandra Sanguinetti, Rinko Kawauchi and Pieter Hugo. This year, portraits by Hassan Hajjaj have been selected to be shown alongside the works in the *Taylor Wessing Photo Portrait Prize*.

Hassan Hajjaj's first encounter with photography came through the local portrait studio in his home city of Larache, north-west Morocco, where he was born in 1961. Visiting the photography studio was a rare but celebratory event: 'your mum would dress you in your best clothes, and even put perfume on you,' Hajjaj explains. Surrounded by backdrops and props, he posed for portraits with his family, the resulting prints were shared with relatives or sent to his father who was living in London. Hajjaj recalls, 'I probably sat for five or six photographs before I came to England.'

At the age of 12, Hajjaj and his family joined his father in London. As a Moroccan boy who didn't speak English, it took time for Hajjaj to settle. 'Growing up in London, we felt like foreign kids in a new land, trying to adjust.' He became interested in the city's hip-hop, soul and reggae scenes, and after leaving school, began organising and promoting underground club nights and parties, and assisting friends on fashion shoots and with music videos. By 1984, he had opened a shop on Neal Street, Covent Garden named R.A.P. (Real Artistic People), which sold Vivienne Westwood and John Galliano creations alongside his own streetwear designs, as well as vinyl records and tickets to music events. R.A.P. became a space where people from all different backgrounds would gather. 'I probably didn't understand the importance of what we were doing at the time, we were just doing our own thing, but it was a golden moment to be part of. It was exciting, it was raw, it was naïve.'

During this time, he first picked up a camera and began photographing visitors to his shop. Friends who studied art, music and fashion all became his subjects. Now, looking back, he admits, 'I was meeting all these interesting people and I wanted to capture them – to freeze them in time.' One of those friends was British-Caribbean artist Zak Ové, who was studying at Saint Martin's School of Art, and the two began collaborating on creative projects. Hajjaj bought Ové's Pentax MX 35mm film camera, and continued to use it well into the 2000s. He recalls a key moment in their friendship, which laid the foundation for his career as an artist: 'Zak saw me taking pictures, and bought me a wide angle lens as a birthday present. I remember it cost a lot of money, and I thought, I need to start taking photographs properly now.'

Hajjaj now uses a digital camera, but his approach to photographing his sitters remains consistent. Despite having the appearance of studio portraits, 'all my shoots are done in daylight, and most of them take place on the street,' Hajjaj explains.

The ambience on Hajjaj's photo shoots is always convivial. 'Ultimately,' he says, 'I want everyone to have a memorable day. There's music, there's food, there's chaos,' he continues, 'there's too many people, and too many props out, but everything is planned.' Hajjaj always works out compositions for the portraits in advance – 'usually I make a little drawing beforehand' – but, as the shoot unfolds, he 'goes with the flow,' giving sitters the space to explore poses and try different outfits he prepares.

Hajjaj styles the photoshoots, selecting colourful patterned backdrops made from market fabrics or inexpensive rugs that are ubiquitous throughout Morocco. Outfits are put together by Hajjaj too. Sometimes he responds to the sitter's own clothes, adding only a few accessories – Moroccan babouche slippers, branded socks,

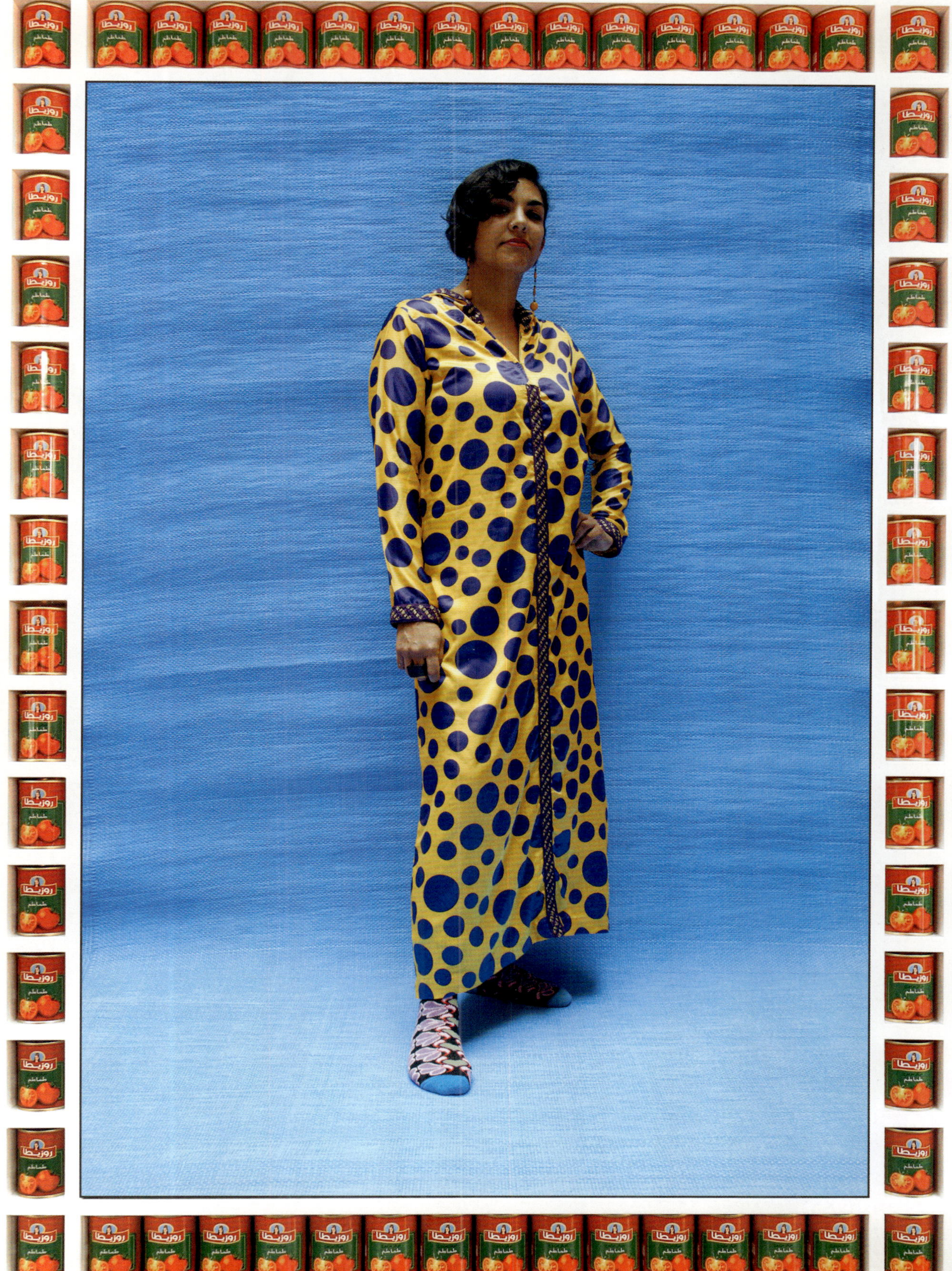

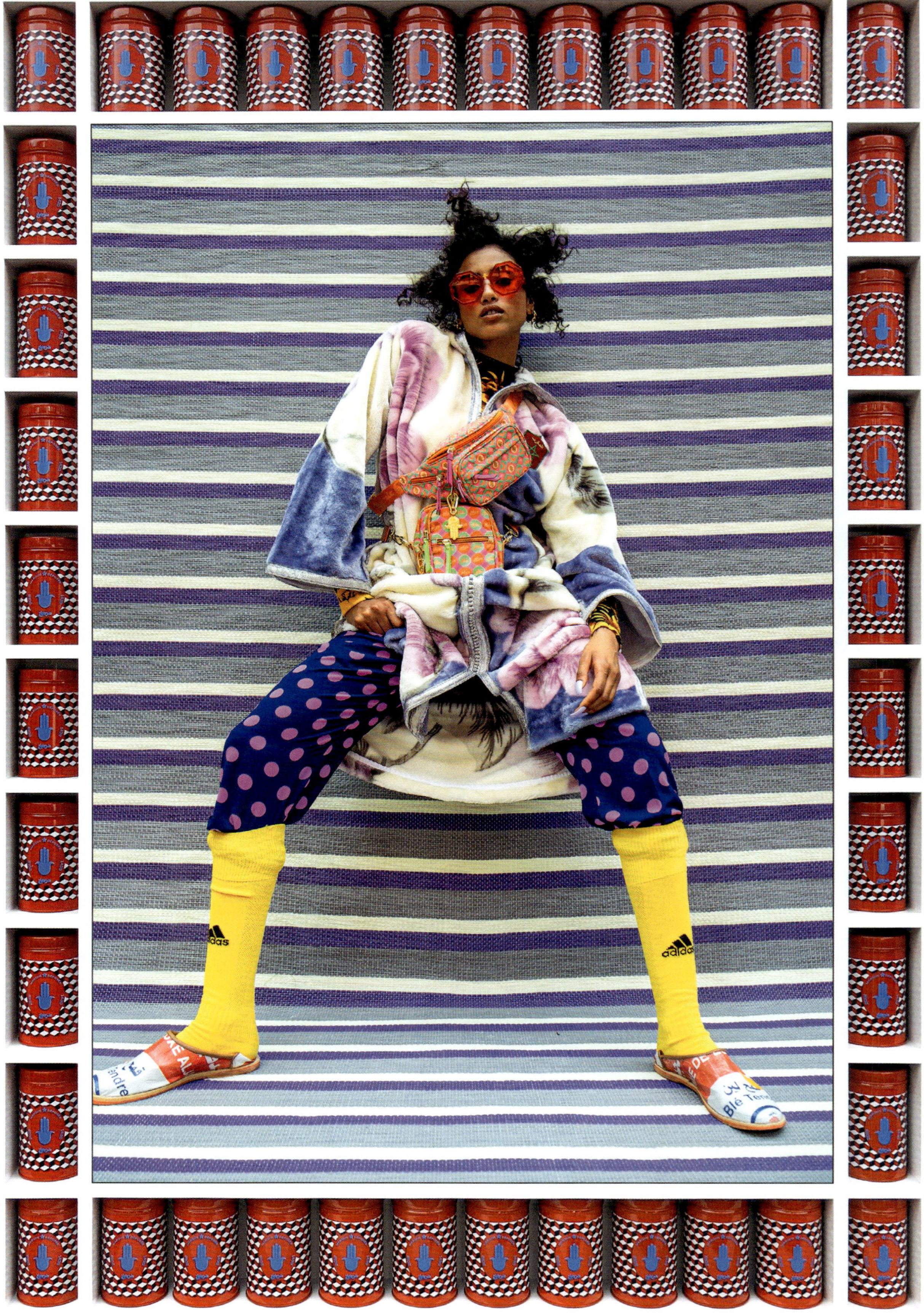

Hassan Hajjaj

Previous page
Heba Amin, 2013 / 1434
Opposite
Imaan, 2020 / 1442
From the series *My Rockstars*
Framed chromogenic prints

kitsch sunglasses from Camden market, for example – but he also styles complete 'looks' for each sitter, using outfits he has designed. When visiting markets in London and Morocco he buys fabrics that are then transformed by tailors and artisans in Marrakech, according to Hajjaj's designs. The outfits blend traditional silhouettes – kaftans, suits – with clashing colours and bold patterns, and incorporate recognisable, often counterfeit, Western fashion branding.

In contemporary photography, frames can often be an afterthought, secondary to the image, but for Hajjaj they are a vital element of the finished work. He likens his pieces to 'historical paintings in their golden frames, which were made specifically for the work.' Surrounding his images are custom-made frames, inset with recognisable objects – tomato-shaped ketchup bottles, cans of drinks from Western brands, or Moroccan market products – repetitively displayed in grids to evoke 'decorative Moroccan mosaic patterns.'

Throughout Hajjaj's work, there is a sense of existing between cultures. Even the act of dating his artworks – which feature both the European Gregorian calendar date and the corresponding year in the Islamic Hirji calendar – is a way for Hajjaj to express his dual identity and 'remind myself where I have come from.' Having spent much of his life travelling between Morocco and London, his work playfully explores the cultural, commercial and social phenomena that emerge at the intersection of these British and North African cultures.

In the late 1990s, Hajjaj started exhibiting his work in London and Marrakech, and began his most enduring photographic project, *My Rockstars*, a homage to the people who inspire him. The series features portraits of 'friends, or friends of friends, or people who I meet along the way on my travels.' *My Rockstars* began in 1998 and is still ongoing, with Hajjaj preferring to work in long-term open-ended projects. Over three decades, his 'rockstars' have expanded to include different fields of achievement, 'from a boxer, to a musician, and a painter, photographer, and on and on. That's the idea.'

As his profile has grown outside the UK and Morocco, his sitters have also become more international, and he has photographed in the streets of New York, Los Angeles, Paris and Dubai for the *My Rockstars* project. Familiar faces, such as Hollywood actor Will Smith and singer Alicia Keys, feature alongside British painter Lynette Yiadom-Boakye, British-Ghanaian fashion designer Joe Caseley-Hayford and other figures, such as Moroccan singer Hindi Zahra or British artist Blaize Simon, who may be less well known. For Hajjaj, the series is about reclaiming the idea of what a rock star is. 'I'm trying to break the mould and own the word, and I'm highlighting people that sometimes don't get seen in the mainstream.'

For Hajjaj, the significance of the series lies in the way the portraits 'preserve a record of the time, the places, the people and the style.' He notes, 'I always say, anybody can hang a piece of cloth and take a picture against it. It's the easiest thing. But at the end of the day, what are you trying to say with a portrait?'

Included in this year's In Focus display at the National Portrait Gallery are four portraits from *My Rockstars*, made between 2013 and 2021, in which Hajjaj spotlights inspiring creatives from North Africa. Having photographed people across the globe, Hajjaj explains, 'for this In Focus display, I decided to show my region.'

The earliest of the portraits depicts Egyptian diasporic artist and educator Heba Amin (p.73), photographed in 2013, whose work explores technology and power dynamics in the Middle East. Hajjaj notes, 'I met her many years ago, and admire her as an artist.' Also featured is Imaan

Hassan Hajjaj
Style Beldi, 2020 / 1442
From the series *My Rockstars*
Framed chromogenic print

Hammam (p.74), a Dutch model of Moroccan and Egyptian heritage, who Hajjaj photographed for *Vanity Fair* magazine. His styling for this portrait is a prime example of how Hajjaj elevates everyday materials. 'Imaan's djellaba robe is made from cheap blankets, used in most African countries in the winter, which will be very familiar to local people,' he explains, 'but I'm trying to make them look as good as a Versace outfit, like something a rock star would wear.'

Karim Chater, also known as Style Beldi (p.77), is a Moroccan artist and stylist who has become a social media sensation for combining vintage Moroccan fashion with modern styling. Hajjaj explains that his adopted moniker *beldi* is a word used in Morocco to mean 'something very local, very traditional.' The suit he wears is made from plastic bags, featuring slogans professing love for Moroccan cities. Hajjaj says, 'I thought that if I ever got an opportunity to photograph Karim, I would save this outfit for him.'

Posing atop a motorbike and covered in designer logos, Moroccan rapper and music producer Draganov (p.78) looks every inch the rock star. His outfit is inspired by the leather suits worn by American musicians like Elvis in the 1960s, and is updated with the Louis Vuitton logo. 'Because Draganov is from a new generation, I wanted to play with a modern fashion brand,' he explains. Hajjaj is a fan of the musician, known for his experimental, genre-crossing music, and the pair collaborated on Draganov's visual album, *Colors*, in 2021.

Hajjaj typically uses a wide-angle lens to make his portraits and photographs from a low angle, to bestow a sense of monumentality to his sitter. When on display, his framed works are placed higher than eye level on the wall to reinforce the feeling of looking up at the subject. His inspiration for this point of view comes from a variety of sources, notably martial arts films, whose camerawork often features this perspective, and the music videos he grew up with – 'Hype Williams was a big director who would shoot videos in this way,' Hajjaj notes. Fashion and style publications were also key: 'I was a big magazine nerd and was always buying *The Face*, or *Arena*, *I.D.*, all those magazines, and I always loved the old *Vogue* photography.'

Hajjaj's work is often compared to well-known African photographers of the mid-twentieth century, but what marks his work out, he suggests, is the internationality of his subjects. 'Malick Sidibé, for example, would be shooting people in his city, in his studio. But I'm part of a new generation; I've been able to move around the globe and capture many different people in different countries, different locations.' *My Rockstars* makes visible the increasingly interconnected, globalised world we live in today.

The fifth and final work included in this year's In Focus display is a group portrait of *Keshmara*, or henna girls, from Marrakech (p.80). At the centre of the portrait is Karima, a long-standing collaborator for Hajjaj and the subject of his first feature-length film, *Karima: A Day in the Life of a Henna Girl* (2015). Karima is pictured alongside her cousin, aunt and friends, who all earn a living applying henna in Jemaa el-Fnaa, the main square in the city's medina. Hajjaj remarks, 'they are artists, just using different materials.' The group were photographed in Marrakech, wearing their own clothes, 'I just added the sunglasses and bottles,' Hajjaj notes.

The portrait belongs to another of Hajjaj's series, *Vogue: The Arab Issue: Spring Collection 2048*, an ongoing project which he began around the millennium, inspired by his experience assisting on an *Elle* magazine photo shoot in Marrakech. He was struck by the fact that all the models, stylists and make-up artists were from the West,

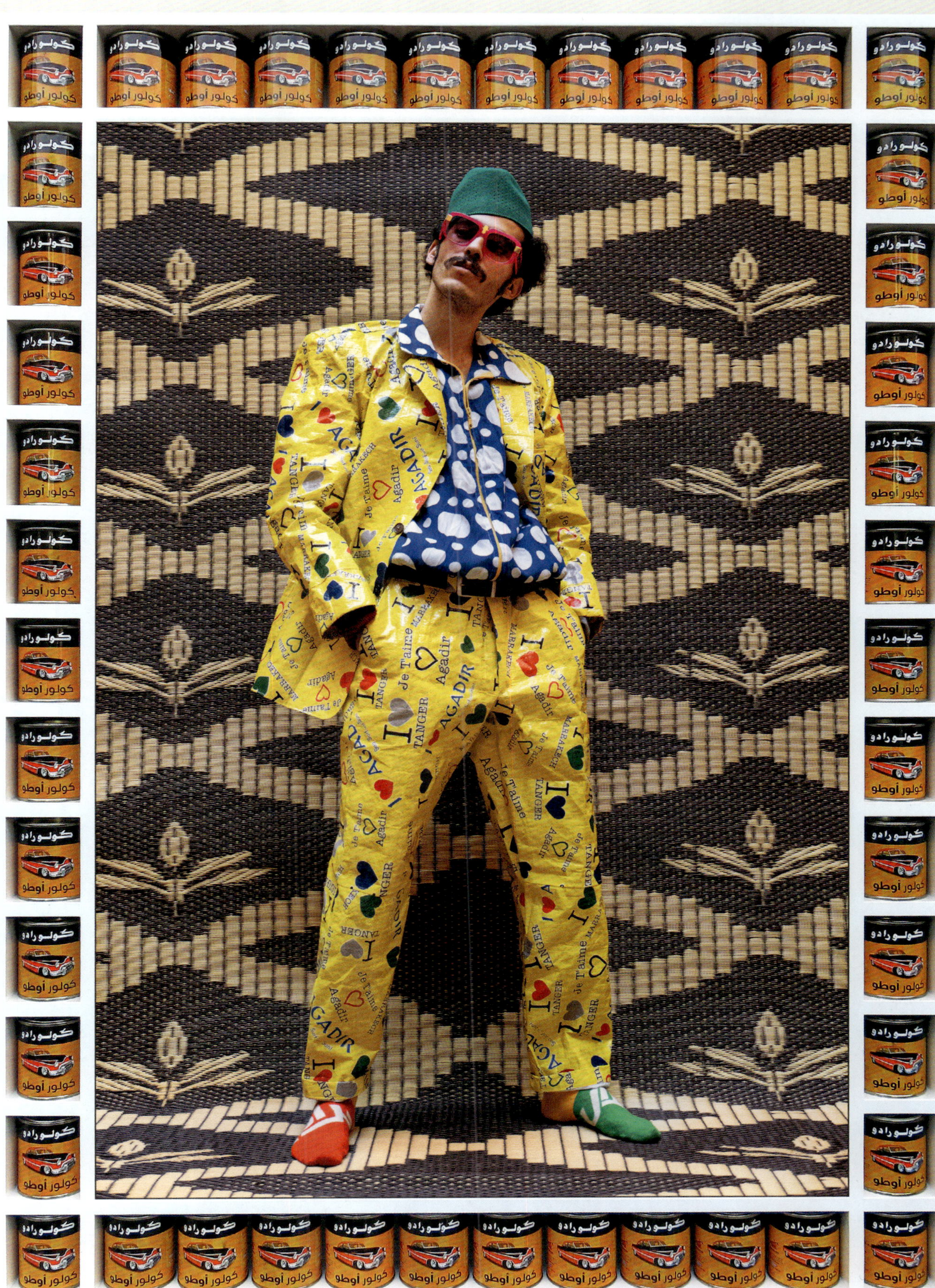

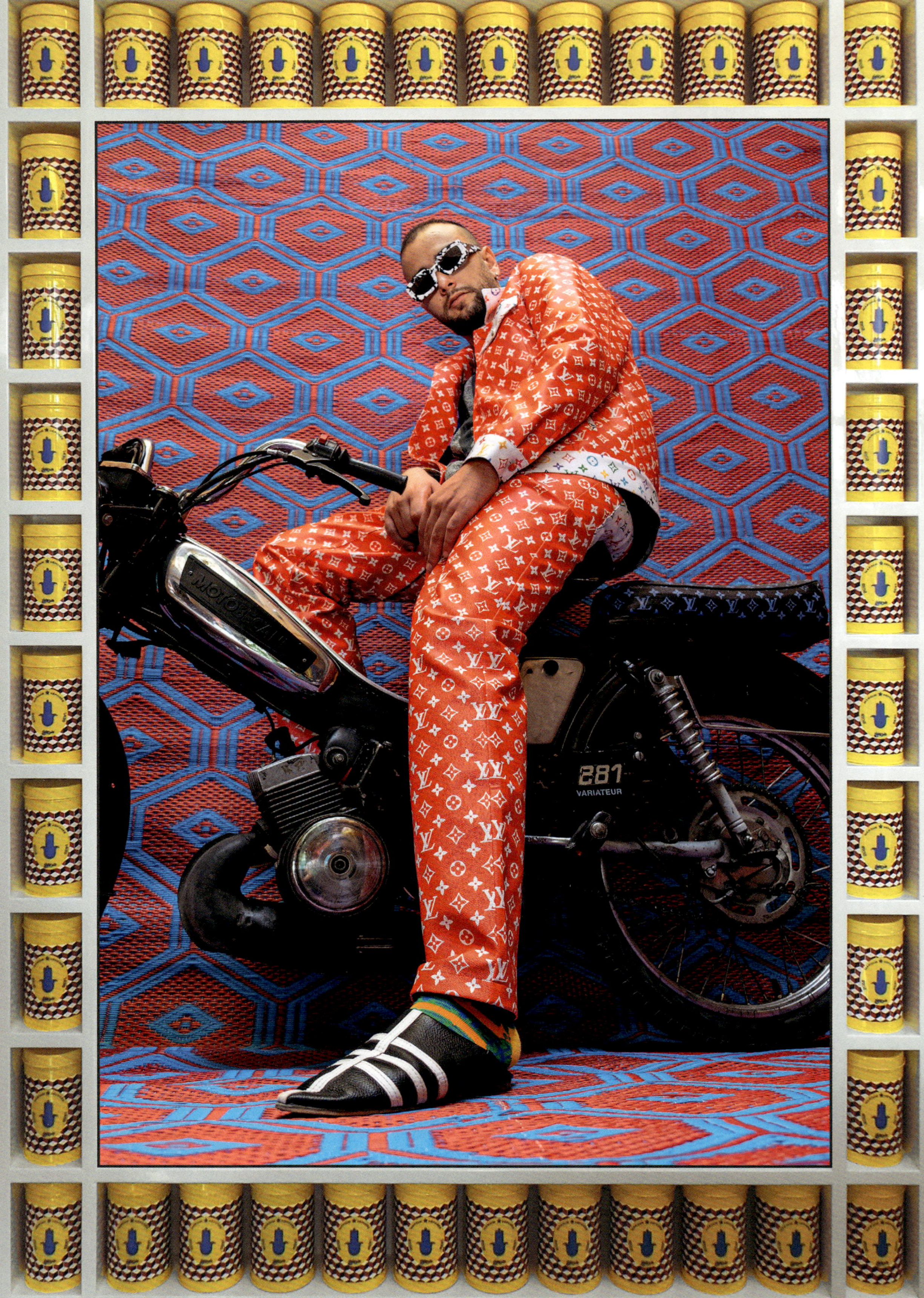

and Marrakech was reduced to an 'exotic space' being culturally appropriated as a backdrop for Western fashion. His frustration was compounded by an awareness that his friends in London also had a very narrow view of Moroccan culture. Hajjaj felt compelled to show his friends a more nuanced picture of where he came from.

He resolved to use his photography to celebrate Moroccan culture, showcasing creatives from the North African diaspora, and subverting stereotypes of his home country in the process. Casting henna girls, dancers and friends in the place of professional models, he created his own fashion shoots around the streets of Marrakech. The series later came to be called *Vogue: The Arab Issue*, the title purposely open to interpretation – does it reference an issue of a monthly fashion magazine, or suggest that superficial exploitation of Arabic culture is an issue that requires attention? Hajjaj allows his viewers to reach their own conclusions.

Hajjaj's work is held in major international collections, including Tate and the Victoria & Albert Museum in London, as well as the Brooklyn Museum and Los Angeles County Museum of Art, and he has staged large-scale museum exhibitions across America, England and France. As someone who, as a teenager, felt that museums 'didn't cater for people like me,' he is always conscious to ask himself and the institution, 'how can I get people who thought like me to come and see the work? How can my work communicate with these people?'

The answer is perhaps the multiple layers of Hajajj's practice, which come together in the 'salons' he creates when exhibiting work. These are environments that feature his framed portraits, but also include seating made from Coca Cola crates, or rugs and lanterns from Moroccan markets, and are often animated by performances and music. For Hajjaj, they make the experience of visiting a museum more inclusive, as they 'catch

the eye of people who might otherwise not be interested in art.' He explains, 'whether it's the branded clothes, or the canned products in the frame, or a portrait of someone who looks like them, there is something that can communicate with them. Once you've caught their attention, then hopefully they will look at all the other layers of the work.'

Hajjaj remains very aware that not all his peers have been given chances to achieve the level of success that he has found. Remembering his early years in London, he recalls, 'there was a lot of great talent around me that never made it, because no record company or fashion brand would give them the opportunity. There were so many talented people in London who were never able to break through.'

He now is making it his mission to give a platform to other creatives. 'I want to be opening doors for the next generation,' Hajjaj explains. In 2018, he curated an exhibition of emerging Moroccan photographers, *Mi Casa Su Casa*, at Comptoir des Mines Galerie in Marrakech, which was restaged in New York in 2022. He is also currently in the process of converting Riad Yima in Marrakech into a multi-purpose space, with a tearoom and boutique selling his own designs and products, and a studio and exhibition space that he shares with the local community. 'I want to present more from the region,' says Hajjaj, 'I believe in the region – and it has believed in me.'

Interview by Sabina Jaskot-Gill

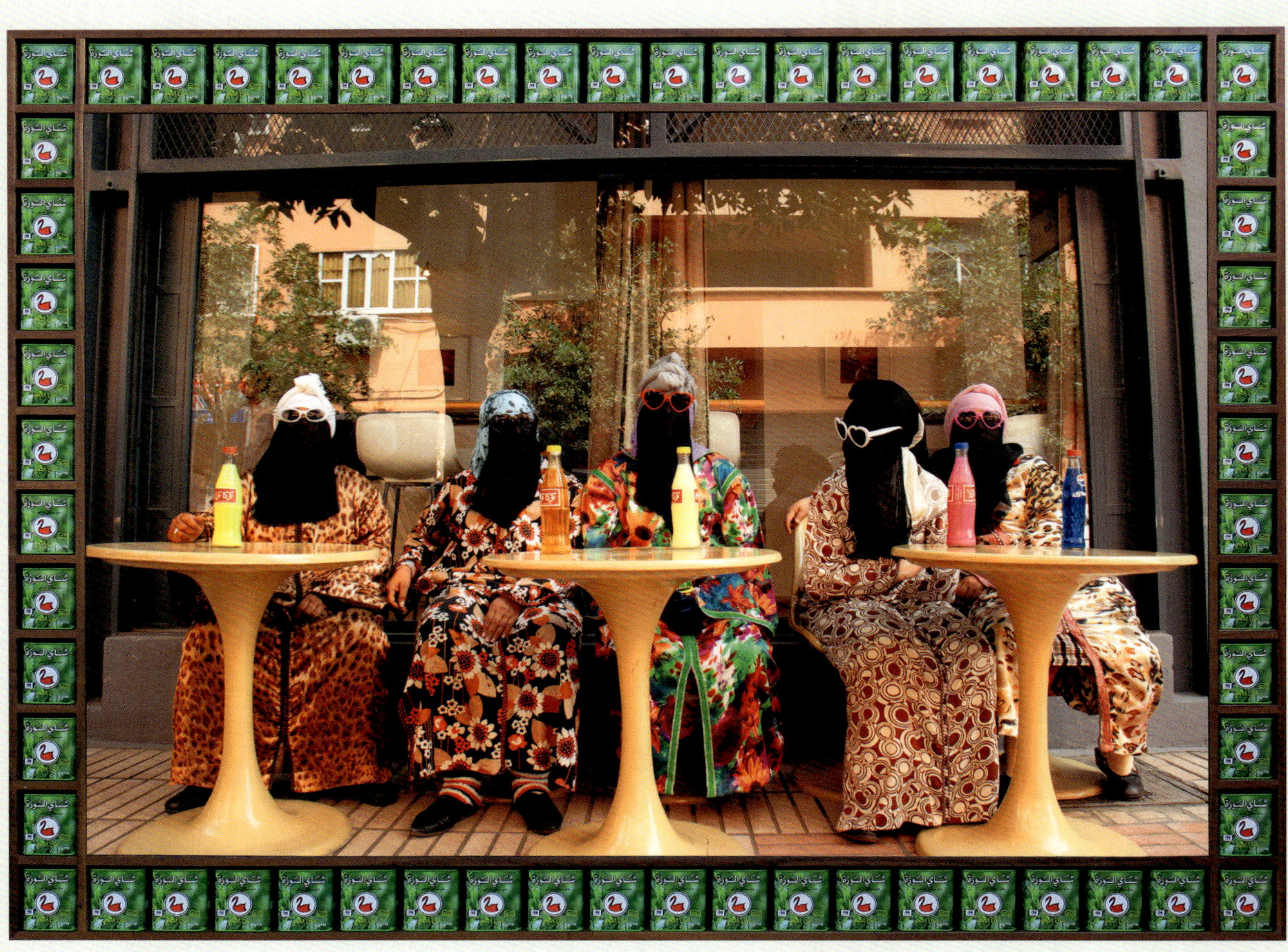

Hassan Hajjaj
Keshmara, 2010 / 1431
From the series *Vogue: The Arab Issue:*
Spring Collection 2048
Framed chromogenic print